THUCYDIDES BOOK I

THUCYDIDES BOOK I

☙

A STUDENTS'
GRAMMATICAL
COMMENTARY

H. D. Cameron

The University of Michigan Press
Ann Arbor

Copyright © by the University of Michigan 2003
All rights reserved
Published in the United States of America by
The University of Michigan Press
Manufactured in the United States of America
⊗ Printed on acid-free paper

2009   2008   2007   2006   5   4   3   2

A CIP catalog record for this book is available from the British Library.

Library of Congress Cataloging-in-Publication Data

Cameron, H. D. (Howard Donald), 1943–
      Thucydides Book 1 : a students' grammatical commentary / H.D. Cameron.
           p.   cm.
      Includes bibliographical references.
      ISBN 0-472-09847-0 (cloth : alk. paper) — ISBN 0-472-06847-4 (pbk. : alk. paper)
      1. Thucydides. History of the Peloponnesian War. Book 1.   2. Thucydides—Language.
3. Greek language—Grammar. I. Title: Thucydides Book one. II. Title.

PA4461.C28   2003
938'.05—dc22   2003055997

ISBN 978-0-472-09847-7 (cloth : alk. paper)
ISBN 978-0-472-06847-0 (pbk. : alk. paper)

PREFACE

❧

For the first-time reader of Thucydides, considerable detailed guidance is needed, as I discovered some years ago when teaching Book I to seniors and graduate students. The older school commentaries, as my students found, were distressingly stingy with grammatical help. It was necessary to provide them with grammatical notes, which over the years eventually evolved into the present commentary. It reflects the practical needs of American advanced students of Greek.

My understanding of Thucydides springs from a four-by-six-inch index card scribbled out for me many years ago by W. R. Connor. At the time, we were both young instructors at the University of Michigan, and I sought his advice on how to teach Thucydides. Just as in a Picasso drawing, it was all there in a few deft strokes.

I thank my students over the years, especially Daniel Berman, Antonis Kaldellis, Amanda Kraus, Dmitri Nakassis, William Short, Josh Ward, and Timothy Allison, who have corrected typos, spotted false accents, and told me to clear up muddled explanations. I am grateful to John Lobur for his careful eye and wise critiques. My thanks also go to colleagues who have used drafts of this commentary in their own classes: Kathryn Morgan (University of California, Los Angeles), Robert Ketterer (University of Iowa), and Sara Forsdyke (University of Michigan). Further, I thank the anonymous readers of the University of Michigan Press for their excellent suggestions and corrections, and I especially thank Collin Ganio of the Press for his encouragement and professional expertise. Thanks also to Marilyn Scott for her keen eye, and to Mary Hashman my editor at the Press.

CONTENTS

ᴜᔓ

CONVENTIONS
AND ABBREVIATIONS

୭ଽ

This commentary is meant to be used with the Oxford Classical Text of Thucydides, edited by Henry Stuart Jones, and with Smyth's *Greek Grammar*, which almost never fails to illuminate Thucydidean syntax. It is also meant to be used with the abridged edition of Liddell and Scott's *Greek–English Lexicon*, which reliably contains nearly all of the vocabulary of book I of Thucydides. My commentary regularly refers to the unabridged lexicon of Liddell, Scott, and Jones to authenticate lexical usage.

I make no claim of elegance for the translations in my commentary. They are meant to illuminate the Greek syntax, and I have not hesitated to use clumsy "translationese" if that would best suit the purpose. Once the grammatical labyrinth is understood, the student should be urged to retranslate into smoother English prose. For elegance, I recommend the 1998 translation by Steven Lattimore.

I have employed the standard chapter numbers used by all modern editions of Thucydides. The origin of this numbering is the 1696 Oxford edition by John Hudson (1662–1719).

The following abbreviations are used for citations in this book.

Buck, *Comp. Gr.*	C. D. Buck. *Comparative Grammar of Greek and Latin.* Chicago: University of Chicago Press, 1933.
Classen and Steup	J. Classen and J. Steup. *Thukydides erklärt van J. Classen.* 5th ed. revised by J. Steup. Vol. 1, *Einleitung: Erstes Buch.* Berlin: Weimannsche Buchhandlung, 1919.
Crawley	Richard Crawley, trans. *The Peloponnesian War,* by Thucydides. Revised by T. E. Wick. New York: Modern Library, 1982.
Denniston, *Gr. Part.*²	J. D. Denniston. *The Greek Particles.* 2d ed. Oxford: Clarendon, 1954.
Gomme	A. W. Gomme. *A Historical Commentary on Thucydides.* Vol. 1, *Introduction and Commentary on Book I.* Oxford: Clarendon, 1956.
Goodwin-Gulick	W. W. Goodwin. *Greek Grammar.* Revised by C. B. Gulick. New York: n.p., 1930.
Goodwin, *Moods and Tenses*	W. W. Goodwin. *Syntax of the Moods and Tenses of the Greek Verb.* Boston: n.p., 1890.
Kühner-Gerth	R. Kühner. *Ausführliche Grammatik der Griechischen Sprache.* Part 2, *Satzlehre.* 2 vols. Bernhard Gerth. Hannover and Leipzig: n.p., 1898.
Lattimore	Stephen Lattimore, trans. *The Peloponnesian War,* by Thucydides. Indianapolis: Hacket, 1998.
LSJ	H. G. Liddell and Robert Scott. *A Greek–English Lexicon.* Revised by Sir Henry Stuart Jones with the assistance of Roderick McKenzie, with a supplement. Oxford: Clarendon, 1968.
Marchant	E. C. Marchant. *Thucydides Book I.* 1905. Reprint, with a new introduction and bibliography by Thomas Wiedemann. Bristol: Bristol Classical Press, 1982.
OCT	H. Stuart Jones. *Thucydidis Historiae.* Edited by Henry Stuart Jones, revised by

	J. E. Powell. 2 vols. Oxford: Clarendon, 1942.
Schwyzer	Eduard Schwyzer. *Griechische Grammatik*. Vol. 1, *Allgemeine Teil, Lautlehre, Wortbildung, Flexion*. 3d ed. Munich: C. H. Beck'sche Verlagsbuchhandlung, 1959.
Schwyzer-Debrunner	Eduard Schwyzer. *Griechische Grammatik*. Vol. 2, *Syntax und Syntaktische Stilistik*. 2d ed. completed and edited by Albert Debrunner. Munich: C. H. Beck'sche Verlagsbuchhandlung, 1959.
Sm.	Herbert Weir Smyth. *Greek Grammar*. Revised by Gordon Messing. Cambridge: Harvard University Press, 1956.
Warner	Rex Warner, trans. *History of the Peloponnesian War*, by Thucydides. With introductions and notes by M. I. Finley. Harmondsworth: Penguin Books, 1954. Reprint, 1972.

INTRODUCTION

உ௫

The first book of Thucydides is a compact masterpiece. Here he sets up the conditions that led to the outbreak of the Peloponnesian War in 431 B.C. With great economy, he gives the reader an analysis of the origins of large-scale wars; integrates a sketch of the historical background into the larger thematic threads of his narrative; presents a brief statement of his methods and goals; outlines a hierarchy of causation; develops a theory of character and human nature; presents a theory of leadership, chance, and foresight; sets up the contrast between a land power and a sea power; and does so within a narrative structure that perfectly focuses these elements. His general theme is the universal and enduring character of laws of international power.

A BRIEF HISTORICAL INTRODUCTION

Colonization

From prehistoric times, the Greeks were on the move. In successive waves, the branches of the Hellenic people—the Aeolians, the Ionians, and the Dorians—migrated, united by religion and a common language but different in cult and dialect. From mainland Greece, the Aeolians and Ionians settled the western coast of Asia Minor. Athens and their relatives in Ionia maintained a loose connection based on a common dialect, the worship of the Delian Apollo, and the tradition of descent from his son Ion. About 1000 B.C., the Dorians spread through the Peloponnese and the southern Aegean Islands, a movement mythologized as the "Return of the Heraclidae." From roughly the middle of the eighth century to the middle of the seventh, the cities of mainland Greece sent out settlements and founded colonies from the Crimea in the Black Sea to Marseilles in what is now France. They settled southern Italy and Sicily, with Ionian colonies, such as Leontini, in the north of Sicily and with Dorian cities, such as Syracuse, in the east and south. The opposition and rivalry between Dorians and Ionians is a major theme in Thucydides' narrative. A colony maintained informal and formal connection with its mother city (μητρόπολις). For instance, the annual magistrates of the Corinthian colony Potidaea, on the westernmost prong of the three-pronged Chalcidice peninsula at the northern end of the Aegean Sea, were sent out each year from the mother city Corinth.

The Ionian Revolt

Their ancestral connection with the Ionians led the Athenians to come to the aid of their relatives in the Ionian Revolt of 499 B.C. The Ionian cities of Asia Minor had become subject to the Lydian Empire of Croesus, and with his defeat, they became subject in turn to the Persian Empire. The Athenians had aided in the burning of the Persian provincial capital, Sardis, and after the revolt was suppressed, the Persians mounted a punitive expedition against Athens, which was repulsed in the famous battle of Marathon in 490 B.C.

The Persian Invasion

Ten years later, when Xerxes was king of Persia, he mounted a massive invasion of Greece in retribution, crossed the Hellespont on a bridge of ships, drank dry the rivers of Thrace, was delayed temporarily by three hundred Spartans under Leonidas at the bottleneck pass of Thermopylae, and marched overwhelmingly into Attica, destroying Athens and dismantling its walls. But during the previous ten-year interval, Themistocles had come to preeminence. He had convinced the Athenians to use the windfall of a newly discovered vein of silver in the mines at Laurium to build ships. He convinced the Athenians to abandon the land to the Persians and evacuate the population by sea to the safety of adjacent islands. By diplomacy, threats, and trickery, Themistocles managed to bring together in a fragile and shaky alliance all the navies of Greece, to defeat the Persian navy in the narrow sea room of Salamis. Xerxes retreated back across the bridge of ships over the Hellespont, leaving his ambitious kinsman Mardonius behind with a residue of the army, and Mardonius was defeated in the final land battle at Plataea in 479 B.C. by an allied army under the command of the Spartan Pausanias.

After the Persian Retreat

Over the objections of the Spartans and Corinthians and following the ingenious policy of Themistocles (Thuc. I.89–93), the Athenians quickly rebuilt their walls, including the fortifications of the harbor, the Piraeus (the Long Walls, connecting the city with the Piraeus, were built later).

Exercising the traditional Spartan right to command, Pausanias led a joint Peloponnesian and Athenian naval expedition, which wrested Byzantium, a Greek colony, from Persian control. But as Thucydides relates (I.94–95), Pausanias was soon discredited, and the Spartans, weary with the burden of the war, withdrew from operations in the Aegean, leaving hegemony to the Athenians, who were only too happy to accept. Under the leadership of Cimon, they, with the aid of their Ionian allies, proceeded to sweep the Persian navy out of the Aegean.

The Delian League

With Athenian leadership, the cities and islands around the Aegean Sea formally organized to counter the Persian threat. The cooperative burden of defense was to be shared, and to the common effort, the members of this league contributed ships or, if more agreeable to them, money. The assessments, whether in ships or money, made for all members of the alliance by the Athenian Aristides were so equitable that he ever afterward enjoyed the nickname "the Just." The money was kept in the shrine of Apollo on the sacred island of Delos. This Delian League, conceived as an alliance for mutual defense against Persia, gradually evolved into the Athenian Empire, in which the members were no longer independent allies but subjects. The studied Athenian policy was to encourage those members who contributed ships to substitute a monetary contribution, until only Lesbos, Samos, and Chios were left with a navy.

As the Persian threat diminished, some members tried to withdraw from the league but were forced to become tributaries. Naxos, for example, left the league but was besieged and forced back into allegiance in 470–469 B.C. Thucydides (I.98) observes that for the first time, a member state lost its independence, contrary to the initial compact of the league, and that the Athenians continued to pursue this policy of reducing members of the league to subjects of Athens.

The Rise and Fall of Cimon

Themistocles, meanwhile, had been ostracized and then condemned in absentia, probably because he was involved somehow in the suspect business of Pausanias. Cimon then became the preeminent political and military leader in Athens. His decisive victory over the Persian navy at the Eurymedon River (467 B.C.) finally eliminated Persian presence in the Aegean.

In 464 B.C., Sparta faced two serious crises: an earthquake and the revolt of the helots, Sparta's large population of slaves, who had retreated to the fastness of Mount Ithome. Cimon's conservative, oligarchical policy was friendly to the Spartans, and he offered to bring an Athenian force to help them. When his offer was rebuffed, he was discredited in Athens and, in 461 B.C., ostracized.

The Rise of Pericles

This was a turning point in Athenian policy. The fall of Cimon was engineered by the democrats under the leadership of Ephialtes and Pericles, and Athens turned anti-Spartan and expansionist. The helots on Ithome held out for years, frustrating Spartan efforts to dislodge them. Finally, in answer to an oracle, the Spartans agreed to allow them to leave the Peloponnesus safely with their wives and children, on the condition that they never return. Pericles cleverly settled them as Athenian colonists at Naupactus, near the mouth of the Corinthian Gulf. Here, then, was an Athenian colony athwart the lucrative trade route to Italy and Sicily.

When Ephialtes and Pericles came to power, it marked a shift from conservative oligarchical policies to democratic policies. One of their first symbolic and practical moves was to reduce the function of the conservative Areopagus from general oversight of the government to their ancestral function as a homicide court. Aeschylus's *Oresteia* was an element in popularizing the move. But it was not approved by all, and Ephialtes was murdered (461 B.C.). Pericles then emerged as the preeminent leader.

Pericles' Constitutional Position

Pericles' formal constitutional position was as a member of the annually elected Board of Ten Generals. Cleisthenes had reformed the Athenian constitution in 508–507 B.C. To break up the old political factions—called the Hill, the Coast, and the Plain—he created ten new political units (tribes, φύλαι) composed of one-third from each faction, so compromise and cooperation within the tribe became necessary. Each tribe annually chose by lot fifty of its members to serve on the βουλή, a kind of executive committee, which saw to the day-to-day operation of the city-state and prepared the agenda for the legislative assembly (ἐκκλησία), the body of all voting citizens. Each tribe annually elected one of its members to the Board of Ten Generals, the military establishment of the city. While the magistrates and other officials came to be chosen by lot, the generals were elected on the basis of competence and thus could be reelected any number of times. While this office was Pericles' constitutional base, his practical political effectiveness came from his forceful personality, his persuasiveness, his admitted foresight, his strategic talent, his recognized integrity, and the general respect that he commanded. As Thucydides puts it, "It was a democracy in word but the rule of its first citizen in fact" (II.65).

From League to Empire

It is something of an oversimplification to say that Athenian policy changed from pro-Spartan to anti-Spartan, but that was effectively what happened. In 454 B.C., the Athenians transferred the treasury of the Delian League from the sacred island of Delos to Athens, claiming that as long as they provided defense against the barbarians, they owed no accounting of the money to the allies (Plut. *Per.* 12 [158]). This is a crucial mark of the transformation from the voluntary alliance for mutual protection, the Delian League, to the Athenian Empire. Thucydides (II.63) has Pericles say to the Athenians in his last speech, "Your empire is now like a tyranny: if you think it was wrong to acquire it, to give it up is outright dangerous."

Athenian Expansion on Land

The period from 461 B.C. to 446 B.C. is sometimes called the First Peloponnesian War, as Athens began effectively to surround Corinth by conquests and alliances, developing something of a land empire. It was short-lived, the advances were lost, and Athenian land expansion came to an end with the Thirty Years' Truce of 446 B.C.

This expansion had begun in 461 B.C. with an alliance with Argos, a traditional enemy of Sparta. Then Megara, the Doric city on the Aegean side of the Isthmus of Corinth, joined the Athenian alliance (459 B.C.). Thucydides (I.103) explains that this was the principal cause of the intense Corinthian hatred (μῖσος) of the Athenians. In 457 B.C., the Athenians won the battle of Oenophyta and conquered their northern neighbors Boeotia and Phocis. Next, the island of Aegina was added to the Athenian Empire (457–456 B.C.), as was Achaea, the territory flanking the south shore of the Corinthian Gulf. At Naupactus, where Pericles had settled the helots, the Athenians established a naval base commanding the mouth of the gulf on its north shore. A glance at the map concluding this book will show how completely Corinth was being surrounded.

The Thirty Years' Truce

The reversal came when the Athenians were defeated in the battle of Coronea in 447 B.C., whereby Athens lost Boeotia. Megara then revolted. The long island of Euboea, which stretches along the flanks of Attica and Boeotia in the Aegean, revolted under the influence of Boeotian intrigue. Euboea, says Thucydides (VIII.96), was, as a base of supply and a refuge, more important than Attica itself, and consequently, its defection was serious enough for the Athenians to seek peace.

By the provisions of the Thirty Years' Truce (446 B.C.), Athens yielded up the territory and alliances it had recently acquired: Nisaea, Pegae, Troezen, and Achaea (Thuc. I.115). Neither side was to attack the other, and neither side was to interfere with the allies of the other. It is argued that a list of the allies of each was appended and that unlisted states were not covered by this provision (cf. Thuc. I.35.2, 40.2). This is a major point at issue between Corinth and Athens in the matter of Corcyra treated by Thucydides in book I.

Thucydides (I.23.5–6) makes a distinction between the unexpressed (ἀφανεστάτην λόγῳ), truest cause (ἀληθεστάτην πρόφασιν) and the expressed causes (ἐς τὸ φανερόν) that led to the breaking of the Thirty

Years' Truce: respectively, namely, Spartan fear of Athenian expansion and the affairs of Epidamnus and Potidaea.

The Affair of Epidamnus and Corcyra

Epidamnus, on the eastern coast of the Adriatic in the vicinity of modern Durazzo, was a colony of the island of Corcyra. It had suffered a series of civil disturbances between the democrats (ὁ δῆμος) and the oligarchs (οἱ δύνατοι), until finally the former expelled the latter. The oligarchs, in turn, with external help from neighboring barbarians, besieged Epidamnus. The besieged democrats sent for help to their mother city, Corcyra, but were rebuffed. On the advice of the oracle at Delphi, the Epidamnian democrats next appealed to Corinth—their grandmother city, as it were, since Corcyra itself had been founded by Corinth. This time, their appeal was successful, because there was bad blood between Corinth and their undutiful colony Corcyra. This led to an odd situation in which Corinth, an oligarchical state, was supporting the democrats in Epidamnus, while Corcyra was supporting the oligarchs. With help from her allies, Corinth put together a navy of seventy vessels to oppose the Corcyrean navy of eighty (Thuc. I.29.4).

The Corcyreans sought arbitration, but the Corinthians refused, which led to the first naval battle between them, off the islands of Sybota in 435 B.C., won by the Corcyreans (Thuc. I.29.5). As the Corcyreans learned that the Corinthians were putting together a Peloponnesian alliance and building ships for a second encounter, they began to be concerned that they themselves were without allies. They had been listed on neither the Athenian nor the Lacedaemonian side in the Thirty Years' Truce. So they sent an embassy to the Athenians seeking such an alliance. The Corinthians, in turn, sent an embassy to persuade the Athenians to refuse, fearing that the Athenian navy would be added to the Corcyrean. The Athenians heard both sides in the assembly and decided for the Corcyreans. This led to a second naval battle off the islands of Sybota (433 B.C.), in which the Athenians played an ambiguous, but active, role. Did this constitute a breach of the Thirty Years' Truce?

The Affair of Potidaea

The affair of Potidaea began with a cautionary measure taken by the Athenians after the naval battle of Sybota (Thuc. I.57.1). On the one hand, Potidaea was a Corinthian colony, situated on the isthumus of

Pallene, the westernmost prong of the three-pronged Chalcidice penin-
sula, and its chief magistrates were sent out annually from the mother city
Corinth. On the other hand, Potidaea was an ally of Athens of the
tribute-paying class, a Dorian city in the Delian League, and therefore
suspect. When the Athenians demanded that they send away the Corinthian magistrates, tear down the walls on the southern side of the city, and
send hostages to Athens to guarantee their loyalty, the Potidaeans revolted. The Corinthians sent a contingent of volunteers to their aid by
land, and the Athenians sent a naval force and a strong force of hoplites,
heavy-armed troops. Eventually the Athenians succeeded in investing the
city by land and sea. The incidents of Corcyra and Potidaea, then, led to
the outbreak of the war.

The Megarian Decree

A third incident, the Megarian Decree, gets less attention from Thucydides. Megara had turned from a traditional relationship with Corinth, and
in 459 B.C., it became an Athenian ally (Thuc. I.103). The Athenians came
to Megara's defense when Corinth attacked them in 458 B.C. But when
Athenian fortunes were reversed in 446 B.C. with the revolt in Euboea,
Megara defected and returned to its alliance with Corinth and the Peloponnesians. By the articles of the Thirty Years' Truce, Athens gave up all the
territorial advances it had achieved in the period of expansion. But the
defection of Megara stuck in Athens's craw, and Pericles issued the Megarian Decree, which interdicted Megara from all the ports of the Athenian
Empire and from the Athenian marketplace itself (Thuc. I.139). Megara's
commercial outlet was toward the Aegean and the East, so this decree
effectively destroyed the Megarian economy.

PRINCIPAL THEMES
Money, Ships, and Walls

The first book of Thucydides' history is about money, ships, and walls.
These three subjects weave their way through the text like counterpoint,
resurfacing again and again. They are the necessary elements that make
large-scale wars possible, according to Thucydides, and they are the secret
of Athenian preeminence and endurance.

    The section called the Archaeology (I.2–19), which treats the early
development of the political and military organization of Greece, empha-

sizes these three things: the need for walled cities for protection against pirates; the safety of the seas guaranteed by the ships of Minos; and the resulting commercial wealth from seaborne trade, which made possible the accumulation of surplus capital. These are precisely the elements necessary for large-scale wars.

The section called the Pentecontaetia (I.89–117), a historical précis of the roughly fifty years between the final retreat of the Persians in 479 B.C. and the outbreak of the Peloponnesian War in 431 B.C., begins with the story of how Themistocles, Thucydides' model of ideal leadership, succeeded by ingenuity, trickery, and alacrity in rebuilding the walls of Athens in the face of Spartan opposition. It was the sagacity of Themistocles that had earlier convinced the Athenians to use the profits from the new-found silver lode at Laurium to build ships in anticipation of the Persian threat. This made it possible for the Athenians in 480 B.C. to take the bold step of taking to the ships, abandoning the land of Attica to the invading Persians.

Finally, in a later day, Pericles, a leader in the Themistoclean mold, adopted the strategy of encapsulating Athens within the Long Walls, abandoning the countryside to the ineffectual Spartan incursions and relying on the sea routes to supply Athens with Crimean wheat. This supply route passed through the narrows of the Hellespont, a geopolitical choke point for Athens. When the Spartans destroyed the Athenian navy at Aegospotami and finally controlled the Hellespont in 404 B.C., cutting off the vital trade route, the Athenians surrendered and the war came to an end. For Themistocles, the money came from the silver mines; for Pericles, the money came from the tribute paid to Athens by the subject cities and islands of the empire.

Causation

Polybius, the later historian of the Punic Wars of Rome, would eventually distinguish three different types of historical causation (3.6–7): pretext (πρόφασις), occasion (ἀρχή), and true cause (αἰτία). These categories are anticipated in Thucydides, although his terms are not as precise as those of Polybius. In Thucydides' account, the Spartans demand that the Athenians drive out the curse of Cylon (I.126), and the Athenians counter with a demand that the Spartans drive out the curse of Taenarus (I.128). These are the pretexts, and Thucydides calls them προφάσεις. The disputes over Corcyra (I.31–55) and Potidaea (I.56–65) and the

Theban attack on Plataea (II.1–7) are the immediate occasions (αἱ λεγόμεναι αἰτίαι) for the outbreak of the war. But according to Thucydides, the true cause (ἡ ἀληθεστάτη πρόφασις) is Spartan fear of Athenian expansion (I.23).

The True Cause—Corinthians

An argument can be made that Thucydides got this wrong. It was not Sparta's interests that were threatened, nor was Sparta eager for war. Rather, the Corinthians bullied, cajoled, and pleaded with the reluctant Spartans to lead a joint Peloponnesian campaign against Athens, because Corinthian interests were being threatened. There is archaeological evidence that in the mid–fifth century, the distinctive Corinthian pottery was being replaced by Athenian pottery in southern Italy, indicating successful Athenian commercial rivalry in the western Mediterranean, traditionally the economic sphere of Corinth. If Corcyra, which lies athwart the sea route from the Corinthian Gulf to Magna Graecia and Sicily, was allied with Athens, the threat to Corinth was severe. The Megarian Decree, by which Corinth's Dorian commercial partner on the Aegean side of the Isthmus of Corinth was interdicted from all trade with the cities of the Athenian Empire, destroyed the economy of Megara. The plight of the Megarians is memorably represented by Aristophanes in the *Acharnians* (524–39, 729–835; cf. *Peace* 605–11).

Spartan and Athenian Character

In Thucydides' account, when the Corinthians speak before the delegates of the Peloponnesian League at Sparta to urge resistance to Athens (I.68–71), they lay out the thematic contrast between Spartan and Athenian character (ἦθος). The Spartans, they say, are naive in foreign affairs, passive, wedded to the status quo, hesitant, lacking in originality. But the Athenians, they say, are always innovators, quick in decision and resolve, risk takers, aggressive, always eager for more (πλεονεξία).

The Speeches

In the forward of his 1629 translation of *The Peloponnesian War*, Thomas Hobbes says Thucydides is "one who, though, he never digress to read a Lecture, Moral or Political, upon his own Text, nor enter into men's hearts, further than the Actions themselves evidently guide him . . . fil-leth his Narrations with that choice of matter, and ordereth them with that Judgement, and with such perspicuity and efficacy expresseth himself that (as Plutarch saith [*Mor.* 347A]) he maketh his Auditor a Spectator." Hobbes continues, "For he setteth his Reader in the Assemblies of the People, and in their Senates, at their debating; in the Streets, at their Seditions; and in the Field at their Battels."

Thucydides is regarded as the objective historian par excellence. Only rarely does he intrude with an opinion of his own (e.g., at I.23). But despite this objective manner, his own interpretation emerges from the speeches and the studied juxtapositions of his narrative. His analysis lies in the speeches, whether they are reports of speeches actually heard or only inventions of Thucydides—as he says (I.22), "what was appropriate to the situation" [περὶ τῶν αἰεὶ παρόντων τὰ δέοντα]. M. I. Finley says, "to lay bare what stood behind the narrative, the moral and political issues, the debates and disagreement over policy, the possibilities, the mistakes, the fears and the motives, his main device was the speech" (introduction to Penguin translation, 25).

Justice, Self-interest, and Gratitude

The assembly debates recorded by Thucydides in book I tend to rest on two thematic pillars of argument: justice (δίκη) and self-interest (τὰ ξυμφέ-ροντα). In the debate at Athens over Corcyra (I.32–43), the Corinthians argue, as a matter of justice, that an Athenian alliance with the Corcyreans would break the Thirty Years' Truce. The Corcyreans, while denying that argument, point out that it is in Athens's interest to have the Corcyrean navy on their side. There is also a variety of the argument from justice, which we may call the argument from gratitude (χάρις), as when the Corinthians remind the Athenians that they once gave them twenty war-ships with which to conquer Aegina (I.41) and that Athens is thus under obligation to them.

πρόνοια, ὀργή, and τυχή

According to Thucydides' account (I.66–78), at the meeting of the Pelo-ponnesian League at Sparta, the Corinthians urge action against Athens, and the Athenians answer with a justification of their empire and a thinly veiled warning about the unpredictable and the accidental in war (τὸ παράλογον, τυχαί). Then, the Spartan king Archidamus, a man of prudent understanding (ξυνετὸς δοκῶν εἶναι καὶ σώφρων), with caution and foresight lays out for the Spartans in executive session (κατὰ σφᾶς αὐτούς) his assessment of the circumstances (I.79–86). As if confirming the Corinthian picture of Spartan character, he urges delay. However, this is not the usual cautious sluggishness (τὸ βραδὺ καὶ μέλλον) that the Corinthians complained about, but the sensible prudence (σωφροσύνη ἔμφρων) that takes time to become realistically prepared. Archidamus argues that the Athenians have wealth and a navy and that it will be strategically futile to invade and devastate Attic land.

By way of contrast with Archidamus's virtue of foresight (πρόνοια), Thucydides introduces the hotheaded jingoist ephor Sthenilaidas (I.86), who dismisses speech making and diplomacy and puts the question by playing on the passions of the assembly. They vote for war. The *pronoia* of Archidamus is trumped by the rashness (ὀργή, I.140) of Sthenilaidas.

Justice versus self-interest; Spartan character versus Athenian character; true cause, pretense, and occasion; foresight versus rashness; the unexpected and the accidental; money, ships, and walls—these are some of the structural themes that Thucydides sets up in book I, and he will ring the changes on them, sometimes ironically, throughout his history.

Thucydides has caught—in the test tube, as it were, of this little war—the fundamental laws of international power. As long as human nature remains the same (κατὰ τὸ ἀνθρώπινον), these patterns will occur again and again. The future statesman who, like a physician, recognizes the symptoms can with foresight ease his city through the crisis. Thucydides justifiably expects us to find his book useful (ὠφέλιμα) and a possession for all time (κτῆμα ἐς αἰεί).

OBSERVATIONS ON
GRAMMAR AND STYLE

ʊʂ

SPELLINGS FAVORED BY THUCYDIDES

ἤν instead of ἐάν
ξύν instead of σύν, both as preposition and as preverb
ἐς instead of εἰς
⁻σσ⁻ instead of Attic ⁻ττ⁻ (e.g., θάλασσα instead of θάλαττα)
⁻ρσ⁻ instead of Attic ⁻ρρ⁻ (e.g., θάρσος instead of θάρρος)
αἰεί instead of ἀεί

SOME FEATURES OF STYLE

Schema Thucydideum. Thucydides often likes to use a neuter participle or a neuter adjective instead of the corresponding abstract noun. E.g., τὸ δεδιός [fear] and τὸ θαρσοῦν [boldness] (I.36.1; Sm. §1025); τὸ πιστόν [confidence] (I.68.1). Such an expression may be modified by a genitive. E.g., τῆς πόλεως τὸ τιμώμενον [the dignity of the state] (II.63; Sm. §2051); τὸ σαφὲς τῶν τε γενομένων καὶ τῶν μελλόντων [the clear truth of what has happened and what will happen in the future] (I.22.4).

Constructio ad sensum. A seeming violation of strict syntax, especially concord, can occur to serve the meaning. E.g., ἡ γνώμη τοῦ Ἀρίστεως τὸ μὲν μεθ' ἑαυτοῦ στρατόπεδον ἔχοντι ἐν τῷ ἰσθμῷ ἐπιτηρεῖν τοὺς Ἀθηναίους [The plan of Aristeus was to keep his army with him on the isthmus and keep an eye on the Athenians] (I.62.3). Here, the genitive τοῦ Ἀρίστεως is modified by the dative participle ἔχοντι as though ἡ γνώμη τοῦ Ἀρίστεως was equivalent to ἔδοξε τῷ Ἀρίστει. The construction may also occur with possessive pronouns and adjectives, as in τὰ ἡμέτερ' αὐτῶν [our own resources] (I.82.1). The αὐτῶν modifies the τὰ ἡμέτερα by a construction according to sense.

The "lilies-of-the-field construction," or prolepsis. "The subject of the dependent clause is often anticipated and made the object of the verb of the principal clause" (Sm. §2182), as in the biblical verse "Consider the lilies of the field, how they grow" [καταμάθετε τὰ κρίνα τοῦ ἀγροῦ πῶς αὔξουσιν] (Matt. 6.28) instead of "Consider how the lilies of the field grow." E.g., Ἦλθε δὲ καὶ τοῖς Ἀθηναίοις εὐθὺς ἡ ἀγγελία τῶν πόλεων ὅτι ἀφεστᾶσι [and immediately there came to the Athenians news of the cities, that they were in revolt] (I.61.1).

Avoidance of parallelism. Logically parallel ideas, which we might expect Thucydides to express in grammatically parallel constructions, are often shifted off target with grammatical variation. For instance, in a μέν . . . δέ construction, the element introduced by δέ may be of a different type from that in the μέν part. E.g., Καὶ τὸ ἄλλο Ἑλληνικὸν ὁρῶν ξυνιστάμενον πρὸς ἑκατέρους τὸ μὲν εὐθύς, τὸ δὲ καὶ διανοούμενον [[I, Thucydides,] seeing the rest of Greece taking one side or the other, some immediately and some thinking about it] (I.1.1): the adverb εὐθύς is balanced by the participle διανοούμενον; [οἱ Κορίνθιοι οὐχ ἡσύχαζον ἀνδρῶν τε σφίσιν ἐνόντων καὶ ἅμα περὶ τῷ χωρίῳ δεδιότες [[The Corinthians] did not refrain from action since they had citizens inside [Potidaea] and also out of fear for the territory] (I.67.1): The two elements joined by the τε . . . καί are a genitive absolute and a nominative participle; (κελεύω) αἰτιᾶσθαι μήτε πόλεμον ἄγαν δηλοῦντας μήθ' ὡς ἐπιτρέψομεν [I advise you] to make our complaints known without either openly threatening war or [suggesting] that we will let them [do as they please]] (I.82.1) and (δύναμις) φέρουσα ἐς μὲν τοὺς πολλοὺς ἀρέτην, οἷς δὲ ἐπαμυνεῖτε χάριν, ὑμῖν δ' αὐτοῖς ἰσχύν [[A power] bringing [to you a reputation for] virtue in the eyes of the world, thanks from those you will defend, and for yourselves strength] (I.33.2): the three grammatically nonparallel, but balanced, constructions are a prepositional phrase, a relative clause, and a dative.

Historical present. The present tense can be used with past meaning. E.g., ὁ δὲ Θεμιστοκλῆς προαισθόμενος φεύγει ἐκ Πελοποννήσου ἐς Κέρκυραν [Themistocles, getting wind [of this], fled from the Peloponnese to Corcyra] (I.136.1).

Qualification of nouns by adverbs or phrases. E.g., ἡ πρότερον ἀπραγμοσύνη [our earlier noninvolvement] (I.32.5); τῷ αὐτίκα φανερῷ [by something apparent at the moment] (I.42.4); τὴν ἀφ᾽ ἡμῶν ἀξίωσιν [the claim we are making] (I.37.1).

Substantives formed by the neuter article. These are often translated by an abstract noun. E.g., τὸ ἐφ᾽ ἑαυτῶν [their own interests] (I.17.1); τὸ λῃστικόν [piracy] (I.4.1).

Hyperbaton. Words that logically belong together may be displaced (Sm. §3028).

> *For emphasis.* E.g., ἀρχαιότροπα ὑμῶν τὰ ἐπιτηδεύματα πρὸς αὐτούς [Old-fashioned are your policies toward them] (I.71.2).
>
> *Inserted explanation.* E.g., ἀνάγκη δὲ ὥσπερ τέχνης αἰεὶ τὰ ἐπιγιγνόμενα κρατεῖν [It is necessary, as in the case of any craft, for innovations always to win out] (I.71.3).
>
> *For rhythmical reasons.* E.g., ἐν τούτῳ δὲ ἐπρεσβεύοντο τῷ χρόνῳ [And during this time they sent embassies] (I.126.1).

Switching prepositions. Thucydides will use two different balanced prepositions for the same meaning. E.g., ἀλλ᾽ οὔτε πρὸς τοὺς ἄλλους οὔτε ἐς ἡμᾶς τοιοίδε εἰσίν [Neither toward the others nor toward us are they like that [honorable]] (I.38.1). Here, πρός and ἐς mean the same.

OUTLINE OF BOOK I

⚘

COMMENTARY

ᘒᖇ

1.1. ὡς ἐπολέμησαν. Instead of using the accusative relative pronoun ὅν referring to τὸν πόλεμον, Thucydides uses an indirect question with a displaced object, literally, "He wrote the war, how they fought." This figure is called prolepsis (literally, "anticipation") or the "lilies-of-the-field construction" (from the biblical verse Matt. 6:28, "Consider the lilies of the field, how they grow" [καταμάθετε τὰ κρίνα τοῦ ἀγροῦ πῶς αὐξάνουσιν]). "The subject of the dependent clause is often anticipated and made the object of the verb of the principal clause" (Sm. §2182).

εὐθὺς καθισταμένου. Genitive absolute expressing time. Notice that in Greek, unlike the Latin ablative absolute, a participle may stand alone without a noun in the genitive when it is obvious what such a noun would be. Sm. §2072. The full expression would be εὐθὺς καθισταμένου τοῦ πολέμου, "the moment the war broke out."

ἐλπίσας. "expecting." Verbs meaning hope, expect, promise, threaten, swear, etc. take the future infinitive in indirect discourse. Sm. §1868.

τεκμαίρομαι. After Homer—i.e., in classical Greek—this verb means "judge from signs or tokens." But here, Thucydides has used it in a special sense, "taking as evidence for this judgment [that it was going to be the greatest war ever] the fact that . . ."

ξυνιστάμενον. Indirect discourse with accusative plus participle after a verb of perception (ὁρῶν). Sm. §2110–12.

τὸ μὲν . . . τὸ δὲ. When used with μέν and δέ without a following noun, the article behaves like a demonstrative. Sm. §1106–7. The combination ὁ μὲν . . . ὁ δὲ means "the one . . . the other," and οἱ μὲν . . . οἱ δὲ means "some . . . and some . . ." Here, it takes up from τὸ ἄλλο Ἑλληνικόν [the rest of Greece], to mean "part of the rest of Greece doing so straightaway, and part thinking about it." We probably should imagine that after διανοούμενον could be supplied ξυνίστασθαι, "considering to join the league."

1.2. ὡς δὲ εἰπεῖν. "so to speak." "Certain idiomatic infinitives are used absolutely in parenthetical phrases to limit the application of a single expression or of the entire sentence" (Sm. §2012, the absolute infinitive). E.g., ὡς ἔπος εἰπεῖν, "so to say"; ἑκὼν εἶναι, "willingly"; ὡς ἐμοὶ δοκεῖν, "as it seems to me."

ἐπὶ πλεῖστον. Here, ἐπὶ with the accusative expresses quantity or measure (Sm. §1689.3c)—as in ἐπὶ μικρόν, "a little," and ἐπὶ πλέον, "still more"—hence, "the most." Here, "of the majority of mankind."

1.3. εὑρεῖν. Epexegetical (explanatory) infinitive—i.e., an accusative of respect that happens to be an infinitive. An accusative of respect (Sm. §1600—1601) is an accusative in the vicinity of an adjective expressing in what respect that adjective is true, as in δεινοὶ μάχην, "terrible with respect to battle." Hence, here, "things impossible with respect to discovery." Note that the infinitive limiting the meaning of an adjective—i.e., an epexegetical infinitive—is commonly active (or middle) where English often expects a passive (Sm. §2006). So one can here translate "impossible to discover" or "impossible to be discovered."

ἐκ δὲ τεκμηρίων ὧν. In Greek, a relative pronoun whose antecedent is either genitive or dative can take its case from its antecedent rather than from its use in its own clause. Logically, one would expect this relative to be accusative plural ἅ, since it is the object of the participle σκοποῦντι and, at the same time, the object of πιστεῦσαι, but it is attracted to the case of its antecedent, τεκμηρίων. Sm. §2522.

μοι πιστεῦσαι ξυμβαίνει. Literally, "to believe happens to me"—i.e., to retranslate, "I happen to believe."

κατά . . . ἐς. Both mean "concerning." LSJ s.v. κατά B.IV.2, s.v. ἐς A.IV.1. Thucydides avoids repeating the preposition κατά and characteristically avoids strict parallelism.

2.2. φαίνεται takes the participles καλουμένη, οἰκουμένη, οὖσαι, ἀπολείποντες, and βιαζόμενοι. Sm. §§2106, 2143.

νεμόμενοι. In the middle, νέμω means "possess, enjoy, or inhabit." LSJ s.v. A.II. Crawley translates, "cultivate."

ὅσον ἀποζῆν. "as much as [necessary] to live off."

ἄδηλον ὄν. Accusative absolute. "A participle stands in the accusative absolute, instead of the genitive, when it is impersonal, or has an infinitive as its subject. When impersonal, such participles have no apparent grammatical connection with the rest of the sentence" (Sm. §2076–78). Hence, "it being unclear when . . ."

ὁπότε. Indirect form of the interrogative adverb, used for indirect questions. The direct form would be πότε. See the chart in Sm. §346; cf. §2664.

τις . . . ἄλλος. "somebody else." Thucydides often separates words that ordinarily go together.

ἀφαιρήσεται. This is the verb of the indirect question introduced by ὁπότε. In the middle, it means "take for oneself/themselves" and would ordinarily have an accusative of the thing and a genitive of the person, as in Thuc. III.58.5: τὰς πατρίους τῶν ἑσσαμένων καὶ κτισάντων ἀφαιρήσεσθε [you will take the ancestral practices away from those who established and founded them]. There is no accusative object of ἀφαιρήσεται because it can be inferred from what precedes—sc., γῆν (brachylogy, Sm. §3018k). After primary tenses, the mood of the original direct question is retained, but after secondary tenses, the mood may change to optative. Sm. §2677. Here, after the secondary leading verb ἀπανίσταντο, Thucydides chooses to retain the indicative. ἀτειχίστων ἅμα ὄντων can be taken either as a genitive absolute or as the genitive after ἀφαιρήσεται. Classen and Steup (ad loc.) prefer the latter.

Notice the connectives in the first independent clause of this sentence. The main verb is ἀπανίσταντο, and dependent on it are five nominative plural participles connected by various coordinate conjunctions, some positive and some negative.

οὐδ' ἐπιμειγνύντες
νεμόμενοί τε
καὶ . . . οὐκ ἔχοντες
οὐδὲ . . . φυτεύοντες
(τῆς) τε . . . ἡγούμενοι

ἂν ἡγούμενοι ἐπικρατεῖν. ἡγούμενοι introduces indirect discourse with accusative and infinitive, but when the accusative subject of the infinitive is the same as that of the leading verb, the accusative is omitted. Sm. §§937, 1972. Hence, "thinking that they . . ." ἂν goes with ἐπικρατεῖν, indicating that in direct discourse, it was a potential optative: ἐπικρατοῖμεν ἄν, "we would obtain . . ." Sm. §§1846, 2023. ἐπικρατέω takes the genitive.

2.3. τῆς γῆς ἡ ἀρίστη. Normally, we would expect ἡ ἀρίστη γῆς, but this is a characteristic mode of expression for Thucydides.

2.4. δυνάμεις τισί. Thucydides, who does not want to talk about cities yet, for that is the point of the discussion, uses such indefinite expressions to mean either territories or persons or both. Hence, "some powers became greater than some [others]" or "some people became greater than other people."

τε . . . ἐνεποίουν . . . καὶ ἐπιβουλεύοντο. The τε . . . καί combination connects the two finite verbs.

ἐμποιέω. When used of circumstances and conditions, this verb means "cause, produce." LSJ s.v. II.3.

ἐπιβουλεύω means "plot against someone (dat.)," and the middle transformation makes the dative the subject, so ἐπιβουλεύομαι means "I get plotted against."

2.5. γοῦν. Combination of γε and οὖν, usually translated, "at any rate." "γοῦν commonly confirms a previous general assertion by giving a special instance of its truth" (Sm. §2830).

ἐκ τοῦ ἐπὶ πλεῖστον. An adverb or a prepositional phrase can be made to serve as a noun by placing it in attributive position after an article. E.g., οἱ νῦν, "the now (men)" (i.e., contemporaries); οἱ ἐν τέλει, "those in office." ἐπὶ πλεῖστον means "over the greatest distance" or "over the longest period of time." LSJ s.v. πλεῖστος IV.3. ἐκ πλείστου means "from the longest time ago." LSJ s.v. ἐκ III.1. This expression seems to be a conflation of the two. Some editors have believed there is a textual problem here and want to read something like ἐκ παλαιοτάτου.

2.6. διὰ τὰς μετοικίας ἐς τὰ ἄλλα μὴ ὁμοίως αὐξηθῆναι. ἐς τὰ ἄλλα means "in other parts of Greece." αὐξηθῆναι is the infinitive of indirect discourse after λόγου—hence, "of the theory that there was not the same increase in other parts of Greece due to immigration [as there was in Attica]." μετοικία means "settlement in Attica" by this interpretation. This reading argues that Attica increased its population by immigration, i.e., by the acquisition of metics. Other editors read μετοικήσεις, "migrations from the original land," instead, arguing that because populations were shifting constantly, other cities in Greece could not grow, whereas Athens, being secure, did not lose population. Gomme translates, "Here is a very good example to prove my point that, owing to the continual shifting of population, the rest of Greece did not advance (in security) as much as Attica."

ὡς βέβαιον ὄν. Accusative absolute introduced with ὡς. Sm. §§2076–78. Usually, only participles of personal verbs in the accusative absolute have ὡς. Here, ὡς with the absolute construction marks the ground of belief on which the agent acts. Sm. §2086d. Hence, "[on the grounds that] it was secure."

μείζω. Predicate accusative. "Verbs meaning *to appoint, call, choose, consider, make, name, show,* and the like may take a second accusative as predicate to the direct object" (Sm. §1613).

ὥστε introduces an expression of result. The two result constructions are ὥστε plus the infinitive and ὥστε plus the indicative. Sm. §§2249–78. ὥστε plus the infinitive is general, marking a possible result, but not an actual one ("so that as a general rule, most of the time, . . ."), as in "he behaved in such a manner as to please his friends." ὥστε plus the indicative is specific, marking a result that actually happened, as in "so as a matter of fact, he actually . . ."

3.1. τόδε. "the following, namely, . . ." τόδε, the subject of δηλοῖ, stands as a pronoun representing the next sentence.

3.2. δοκεῖ δέ μοι takes the following infinitives εἶναι, παρέχεσθαι, καλεῖσθαι, and ἐκνικῆσαι. The clause οὐδὲ τοὔνομα . . . εἶχεν is parenthetical.

καὶ πάνυ. "actually." LSJ s.v. πάνυ 2.

ἄλλα τε καί. "especially." ἄλλα is neuter plural to agree with ἔθνη. Greek does this in a reverse fashion from English, which would have "Pelasgians and others" where Greek would have "others and Pelasgians." The combination here is kindred to the adverbial expression ἄλλως τε καί, "especially." Sm. §2980.

καθ᾽ ἑκάστους. "one by one." LSJ s.v. κατά B.II.3.

3.3. οὐ μὴν οὐδέ. "nor again [and to add to this negative example] . . ." Sm. §§2921, 2768. The following μηδέ negates the infinitive ἀποκεκρίσθαι, as is regular.

ἀντίπαλος was originally used to indicate an opponent in wrestling, then to designate one member of a balanced pair, and then, as here, to mean "corresponding." Here, it is a neuter adjective modifying ὄνομα. "The word order, unusual for Attic prose, seems to be caused by the intention to emphasize ἀντίπαλον" (Classen and Steup, ad loc.).

δ᾽ οὖν. "Thucydides frequently uses this combination of particles when he returns to the main subject of his discourse, after a digression or some subordinate discussion" (Classen and Steup, ad loc.).

3.4. ὡς ἕκαστοι. "each by themselves."

τε . . . καί connects the prepositional phrase κατὰ πόλεις [city by city] and the adjective ξύμπαντες, with Thucydides' characteristic avoidance of strict grammatical parallelism. Both serve to explain ὡς ἕκαστοι [severally]. Hence, "The Greeks, both severally city by city . . . and later as a whole . . ."

ὅσοι ἀλλήλων ξυνίεσαν. ξυν-ῑε-σαν. The present stem of ἵημι has two forms, the long-vowel form ἵη‾ and the short-vowel form ἵε‾. The long-vowel form is used only in the present active singular; the short-vowel is used in all other forms based on the present stem. This is the imperfect third plural active. The verb in this meaning (i.e., "understand") takes the genitive. LSJ s.v. II.3; Sm. §1361. The point is that they had a common language.

πλείω. Neuter plural accusative of the comparative used as an adverb. Sm. §345.

ξυνεξῆλθον ought to be intransitive, but it seems to have στρατείαν as its object. LSJ (s.v. συνέρχομαι II.4) explains στρατείαν as a cognate accusative—hence, "united for this expedition." Notice that the MSS read ξυνῆλθον, and ξυνεξῆλθον is a conjecture by Carolus Gabriel Cobet (1813–89), a Dutch scholar.

4.1. ὧν. This relative incorporates its antecedent (Sm. §2536); i.e., there is no antecedent present in the main clause, but if it were there explicitly, it would have been genitive plural, a partitive genitive after the superlative adjective. Sm. §1315. So the genitive plural seems to serve as the object of the verb ἴσμεν. If this construction were artificially spread out, it would be παλαιότατος τούτων οὓς ἀκοῇ ἴσμεν.

τοῦ . . . ἰέναι. Articular infinitive in the genitive, signifying purpose. Sm. §2032e.

5.1 βαρβάρων. Partitive genitive with the two relative clauses. Hence, "and of the barbarians, those who . . ."

ἐτράποντο. The active τρέπω is the transitive, meaning "to turn something," but the middle τρέπομαι is intransitive, meaning "to turn around."

σφετέρου αὐτῶν. *Constructio ad sensum.* σφετέρου, though a possessive adjective agreeing with the singular genitive κέρδους, in meaning has a plural referent—hence, "belonging to them." The intensive adjective αὐτῶν agrees with it in the genitive, by strict grammar, but is plural because of the meaning, even though, by strict logic, it ought to be singular since it modifies adjectively a singular form. Sm. §§926a, 1202.2b, 1203b.

ἕνεκα καὶ τοῖς ἀσθενέσι τροφῆς. "for the sake of food for the weak [among their dependents]." Smyth does not discuss the true dative with substantives, here τροφῆς, but see Schwyzer-Debrunner, 153.

τι καὶ δόξης. "even carrying some glory [literally, "something of glory"] rather." Cf., e.g., τι δυνάμεως at Thuc. II.49.6 and ἐλπίδος τι at II.51.6.

5.2. δηλοῦσι . . . ὀνειδιζόντων. A tricky sentence, but characteristic of many of Thucydides' syntactic habits.

1. δηλοῦσι has no object, when we would normally expect one. Its "object" is the fact in the previous sentence, sc., that piracy brings no shame.

2. The subjects of δηλοῦσι are τινές and παλαιοί, which are connected by the τε before ἠπειρωτῶν and the καί that precedes παλαιοί. They make clear the fact (that piracy brings no shame).

3. τινές is modified by (a) a partitive genitive, τῶν ἠπειρωτῶν, and (b) the relative clause οἷς κόσμος τοῦτο δρᾶν (ἐστί).

4. οἱ παλαιοί is modified by (a) a partitive genitive, τῶν ποιητῶν, and (b) the present participle ἐρωτῶντες.

5. ἐρωτῶντες takes the accusative of what one asks (τὰς πύστεις) and the genitive of the person asked (τῶν καταπλεόντων), and ἐρωτῶντες τὰς πύστεις is followed by the indirect question εἰ λῃσταί εἰσιν, which defines what the inquiries were. The indirect form of a yes-no question is introduced by εἰ, "whether"—not to be confused with conditional εἰ, "if" (Sm. §2671)—and, after a leading verb in a primary tense, keeps the same mood as the direct question would have had. After a secondary tense, it may change to optative. Sm. §2677.

6. The rest of the sentence consists of two genitive absolutes marked by the two parallel participles ἀπαξιούντων and ὀνειδιζόντων, which are connected by οὔτε and the τε that follows οἷς.

7. These genitive absolutes are introduced by ὡς, which signifies that the substance of the absolutes is the opinion of the poets who question whether they are pirates. Sm. §2086d. In such circumstances, ὡς may be given the preliminary translation "on the grounds that."

8. The genitive noun "subjects" of these genitive absolutes are in fact not genitive nouns but whole relative clauses, sc., ὧν πυνθάνονται [those whom they ask not disclaiming the fact] and οἷς ἐπιμελὲς εἴη [those, to whom it was a concern to know, not reproaching].

9. ὧν πυνθάνονται has an incorporated antecedent (Sm. §2536). πυνθάνομαι takes the accusative of what is learned and the genitive of the person from whom it is learned. Here, the relative

is the genitive of the person from whom it is learned. Hence, "those from whom they learn not disclaiming the fact."

10. οἷς, with an incorporated antecedent, is dative with ἐπιμελές. Why is εἴη optative? The rest of the sentence appears to be in primary sequence, but the past time implied in παλαιοί seems to have taken over this clause, which is optative because it is a relative clause in indirect discourse after ἐρωτῶντες. Sm. §2619. Hence, "and those, to whom it was a concern to know, not reproaching."

A recapitulation of the sentence follows.

> And some of the mainlanders make [this] clear even now, for whom it is a source of pride to do this [piracy] well, as do the old ones of the poets (make it clear) by asking for information [τὰς πύστεις]—whether they are pirates the same way everywhere—from those who put into shore, since those from whom they inquire do not deny the business as unworthy, and those, to whom it is a concern to know, do not reproach [them].

5.3. νέμεται. νέμω means in the active "distribute" and in the middle "possess as one's portion," i.e., "have distributed to one." It came to mean "live, dwell in a place." Then, the middle in an absolute construction, with a country or land as subject, came to mean "be constituted, be maintained." Hence, "many parts of Hellas live according to the old way."

6.2. σημεῖον κτλ. "These parts of Hellas still living thus are a sign of the once similar ways of life in all parts."

6.3. ἐν τοῖς πρῶτοι. "ἐν τοῖς is used before the superlative in all genders and numbers (esp. in Hdt., Thuc., Plato)" (Sm. §1089); i.e., the fixed phrase ἐν τοῖς simply intensifies the superlative. Hence, "the very first . . ." Notice that the words ἐν τοῖς πρῶτοι count almost as one word, since the postpositive δέ, which should be second in any clause, here comes after the πρῶτοι.

ἀνειμένη. Perfect middle participle of ἀνίημι, "let go," here meaning "relaxed."

μετέστησαν. Third plural intransitive root aorist of μεθίστημι, here meaning "changed, shifted." It is inconvenient that the third plural transitive sigmatic aorist accidentally has the same form.

οἱ πρεσβύτεροι is the subject of ἐπαύσαντο, but the flow of the sentence (from the standpoint of the English speaker) is interrupted by οὐ πολὺς χρόνος ἐπείδη. We would feel more comfortable if the order were οὐ πολὺς χρόνος ἐπείδη οἱ πρεσβύτεροι . . . ἐπαύσαντο.

αὐτοῖς. This dative is hard to categorize. We would expect a genitive (i.e., "the older of them"). This dative seems to be Thucydides' stylistic device to avoid two contiguous genitives. In poetry, a plural personal dative can stand alone to mean "among." E.g., Τρώεσσιν [among the Trojans] (Hom. Il. 6.477) Sm. §1531.

ἐπαύσαντο. This intransitive middle, meaning "cease [doing something]" takes the supplementary participle φοροῦντες. Sm. §2098.

ἀφ᾽ οὗ. "because of which, from which cause." Note that ἀφ᾽ οὗ more commonly stands for ἀφ᾽ οὗ χρόνου and means "since, after."

ἀφ᾽ οὗ . . . κατέσχεν. "for which reason this fashion prevailed among [LSJ s.v. κατέχω II.6b] the older Ionians for a long time in accordance with their kinship [with the Athenians]."

6.4. ἐς τὸν νῦν τρόπον is parallel with μετρίᾳ, so that it virtually serves as another modifier of ἐσθῆτι.

ἐς τὰ ἄλλα πρὸς τοὺς πόλλους. "in other matters with respect to the many [or toward the many]."

κατέστησαν. This third plural of the intransitive root aorist κατέστην is inconveniently identical to the third plural of the transitive sigmatic aorist κατέστησα. The transitive aorist means "appoint, ordain, establish." The intransitive aorist means "be or come to be in a certain state."

6.5. λίπα. "with olive oil." This adverb is used by Homer in the phrase ἀλείψασθαι λίπ᾽ ἐλαίῳ [anoint oneself richly with oil] (e.g., Il. 10.577). It is an adverb in ⁻α (like σάφα), related to the neuter s-stem noun λίπος, "fat, grease."

ἔστιν οἷς νῦν. Sm. §§2513–14. From the original nominative phrases ἔστιν ὅστις, "there is someone who . . . ," and εἰσίν οἱ, "there are those who . . . ," there developed "oblique cases"—ἔστιν ὧν, ἔστιν οἷς, ἔστιν οὕς—which function as fixed phrases, as though they were simple genitive, dative, and accusative adjectives meaning "some." Hence, "among some barbarians now" or "among some contemporary barbarians."

πολλὰ . . . καὶ ἄλλα. Internal accusatives after διαιτώμενον, modified by ὁμοιότροπα. Sm. §§1554a, 1573. This gives the translation "one would demonstrate that ancient Greece adopted many other customs similar to the barbarians." But ὁμοιότροπα is sometimes interpreted as a neuter plural used as an adverb (LSJ s.v.), giving "one would demonstrate in many other ways that ancient Greece lives similarly to the present barbarian."

7.1. νεώτατα. The superlative degree of the adverb is represented by the neuter plural accusative of the superlative adjective. Sm. §345.

πλωιμωτέρων ὄντων. Genitive absolute. πλωιμωτέρων is the genitive of the neuter plural πλωιμώτερα, used as an impersonal expression, as Thucydides does frequently. Cf. Thuc. I.8.2, where πλωιμώτερα ἐγένετο means "things became more seafaring" or, more elegantly, "sea communications improved" (Warner). Thus, the genitive absolute means "when once sea communications were better."

ἤδη corresponds to Latin iam and has three possible meanings: (1) "already, by this time"; (2) in contrast to something in the future, "immediately forthwith"; (3) after something has occurred first, "henceforth." Like iam, it can refer to the past, the future, or the immediate present. Here, "seafaring being easier by this time."

πρὸς τοὺς προσοίκους. "against the neighbors." Sm. §1695.3c.

ἕκαστοι. Masculine plural. Without warning, Thucydides has switched from the cities (feminine) to the inhabitants of the cities with the masculine ἕκαστοι.

ἀντίσχουσαν. Intransitive feminine singular active present participle, meaning "rising up, emerging."

ἔφερον. Here, this verb has the special meaning "rob, plunder." LSJ s.v. φέρω A.VI.2.

τῶν ἄλλων. Partitive genitive with the ὅσοι clause.

κάτω. In the context of dry land, ἄνω means "inland, away from the shore," and κάτω means "toward the shore." But in the context of the sea, ἄνω means "seaward," and κάτω means "toward land." Hence, ἀνῳκισμένοι (perfect middle participle) means "built inland." Some editors (e.g., Classen) would read a feminine participle to agree with αἱ δὲ παλαιαὶ (πόλεις). If we keep the masculine, it agrees with ὅσοι and means "migrate upcountry, shift one's dwelling inland."

8.1. Δήλου. The island name Δῆλος is feminine. Sm. §232a.

8.2. Μίνῳ. Genitive singular of a noun stem originally in ⁻ωυ⁻ (like ἥρως). Sm. §267, 267a. In Attic, the genitive is shifted to the o-stem second declension. Hence, *Μίν⁻ωυ⁻ου > Μίνῳ.

ἀνέστησαν. Intransitive root aorist third plural of ἀνίστημι. The transitive ἀνίστημι means "make people emigrate." LSJ s.v. III.A.2. Thus, the intransitive aorist means "be forced to emigrate." LSJ s.v. B.II.2.

ὅτεπερ. "when in fact." The intensifying suffix ⁻περ, "indeed," is there to make clear that Thucydides is referring back to an earlier point (I.4.1)— that Minos was the πρῶτος οἰκιστής.

8.3. ἤδη. "by now."

ὡς πλουσιώτεροι ἑαυτῶν γιγνόμενοι. "as is natural with those who become richer than themselves," i.e., richer than they were before.

ἐφιέμενοι. Present active middle participle of ἐφίημι, which, in the middle, means "desire" and takes a genitive. LSJ s.v. B.II.2.

9.2. The indirect discourse introduced by λέγουσι consists of five infinitive phrases.

> Πέλοπα . . . τὴν ἐπωνυμίαν σχεῖν
> ξυνενεχθῆναι (impersonal)
> τυγχάνειν (parenthetical)
> παραλαβεῖν
> καταστῆναι

Πέλοπα . . . τὴν ἐπωνυμίαν . . . σχεῖν. "[they say] that Pelops had the naming of the country"; i.e., the country was said to be named after him.

δύναμιν περιποιησάμενον. "having acquired power for himself." LSJ s.v. περιποιέω II.1.

ὅμως goes with the participle ὄντα. Sm. §2082. Hence, "even though still being."

ξυνενεχθῆναι. Aorist passive infinitive of ξυμφέρω, used impersonally with the meaning "to fall out well, come to pass" (for someone [dat.]) LSJ s.v. συμφέρω B.III. The accusative neuter subject of this infinitive is μείζω. The dative of advantage is ἐκγόνοις.

ὑπὸ Ἡρακλειδῶν. We would expect an article (ὑπὸ τῶν Ἡρακλειδῶν), but Thucydides often makes this omission. Cf. ὑπὸ Θεσσαλῶν at Thuc. I.12.3. Sm. §1136.

ἐκγόνοις, the dative after the impersonal ξυνενεχθῆναι, is by anacoluthon picked up by the two genitives Εὐρυσθέως and Ἀτρέως, who are the two ἔκγονοι in question, paired by μέν . . . δέ in the two genitive absolutes. καὶ ἐπιτρέψαντος begins a third, nonparallel genitive absolute.

μητρὸς ἀδελφοῦ αὐτῷ ὄντος. "being mother's brother to him." Atreus's sister Nikippe was the mother of Eurystheus.

κατὰ τὸ οἰκεῖον. "in accordance with his relationship." Thucydides often prefers a neuter singular adjective used substantively (Sm. §§1021–29) to an abstract noun like οἰκειότητα. Ἀτρεῖ is the dative indirect object after ἐπιτρέψαντος.

τυγχάνειν . . . θάνατον. Although this is printed as a parenthesis, it is still governed by λέγουσι.

Χρυσίππου. Chrysippus was the son of Pelops and Astyoche (a Danaid) and half brother of Atreus and Thyestes. Their mother, Hippodameia, urged them to kill her stepson Chrysippus, but they refused, so she did it herself.

βουλομένων . . . Ἡρακλειδῶν is a genitive absolute. Hence, "the Myceneans being willing out of their fear of the Heraclidae."

Ἀτρέα παραλαβεῖν is introduced by λέγουσι (I.9.2), and the accusative subject Ἀτρέα is then modified by two participial phrases: (1) δύνατον δοκοῦντα εἶναι and (2) τὸ πλῆθος τεθεραπευκότα. The neuter singular object of the participle, τὸ πλῆθος, is then modified by two defining genitives (Sm. §1310), one a plain genitive (τῶν Μυκηναίων) and the other a parallel relative clause (ὅσων Εὐρυσθεύς). The relative adjective ὅσος, which is the relative used to emphasize number, is attracted to the case of its antecedent (Sm. §2532)—which would be something like ἐκείνων if it were there, but it has been incorporated (Sm. §§2536, 2538). It is also genitive because it is the object of ἄρχω, which takes the genitive.

τοὺς Πελοπίδας μείζους καταστῆναι. This infinitive phrase is an indirect statement after λέγουσι (I.9.2).

A recapitulation in clumsy, but syntactically transparent, English follows.

> Those of the Peloponnesians who have received the clearest evidence by tradition from their ancestors say that Pelops was the first, by reason of accumulation of wealth, which he brought with him from Asia into a land of poor men, once he had achieved power for himself, [and that he] had the naming of the country, although still an immigrant; and [they say] that matters fell out later even better [greater] for his descendants, Eurystheus, on the one hand, having died in Attica at the hands of the Heracleidae, and Atreus, on the other hand, being brother to Eurystheus's mother; and Eurystheus, when he used to go on military expeditions, having entrusted Mycenae and the rule [of it] to Atreus because of his family connection—[they say] Atreus fled from his father over the murder of Chrysippus—and when Eurystheus did not return again, with the acquiescence of the Myceneans out of their fear of the Heracleidae, [they say] Atreus, both seeming to be powerful and also having flattered the common people of the Myceneans and those whom Eurystheus used to rule, assumed the kingship; and [they say] that the Pelopidae ended up being greater than the Persidae.

9.3. τὸ πλέον. Thucydides sometimes uses τὸ πλέον instead of μᾶλλον. Sm. §1068.

9.4. προσπαρασχών. "furnishing in addition."

εἴ τῳ ἱκανὸς τεκμηριῶσαι. Sm. §2354. εἰ does not really introduce a condition here but means "in case, on the chance that, supposing." Hence, "supposing he is sufficient to provide evidence to anybody."

ἐν τοῦ σκηπτροῦ ἅμα τῇ παραδόσει. I.e., Hom. Il. 2.101–8. ἅμα [besides] interrupts the phrase and connects it with the preceding argument. One could translate it "furthermore."

οὐκ ἂν κτλ. Present contrary-to-fact condition with εἰ μή plus the imperfect (εἶχεν) in the protasis and the imperfect (ἐκράτει) plus ἂν in the apodosis. Sm. §2302 ff. Here, we would expect a past contrary-to-fact condition (with aorist indicative in both clauses). However, the imperfect can sometimes refer to continual or habitual past action (Sm. §§2304, 2309b), and it then emphasizes the action's continuity. Since Agamemnon was continuing to rule, the imperfect, rather than the aorist, is used here. Classen and Steup (ad loc.) explain this use of the imperfect differently, arguing that the statement is expressed from the standpoint of Homer, who was narrating it as present.

εἰκάζειν δὲ χρὴ καὶ ταύτῃ τῇ στρατείᾳ οἵα ἦν τὰ πρὸ αὐτῆς. "one can conjecture from this expedition what kind they were before this." Although χρὴ usually means "it is necessary," it is sometimes used in a "less strong sense" amounting to "one can" (LSJ s.v. III). cf. Thuc.II.51.2.

10.1. ὅτι μὲν Μυκῆναι μικρὸν ἦν, ἢ εἴ κτλ. The ὅτι ("because") clause and the εἰ clause are parallel, both giving reasons for doubt. εἰ can be translated "given the fact that . . ." The εἰ clause is causal, expressing Thucydides' real opinion, sc., the real reason one may doubt. Sm. §2246; Kühner-Gerth 2:487, §577.1.

ἀπιστοίη μὴ γενέσθαι. "Verbs and expressions of negative meaning, such as *deny, refuse, hinder, forbid, avoid,* [*doubt*], often take the infinitive with a redundant μή to confirm the negative idea of the leading verb" (Sm. §§2739–40).

οὐκ negates only the ἀκριβεῖ.

10.2. οἶμαι governs a potential condition in indirect discourse, with a double protasis. The direct form of the condition would be εἰ ἐρημωθείη . . . λειφθείη δὲ . . . ἀπιστία εἴη ἄν (the so-called future less vivid). When it is downgraded to an infinitive phrase of indirect discourse after the leading verb οἶμαι, the ἀπιστία εἴη ἄν becomes ἀπιστίαν εἶναι ἄν, and the protases remain the same.

τοῖς ἔπειτα. Adverb in attributive position after the article, which makes it into a noun, meaning "to those people then," i.e., "to future generations." Sm. §1153e.

Ἀθηναίων δὲ . . . ἄν . . . εἰκάζεσθαι. Second potential condition dependent on οἶμαι. Here, the protasis is represented by the genitive absolute, the apodosis by the infinitive plus ἄν.

10.3. εἰκός. This picks up the idea of the beginning of the chapter—that is what the resumptive οὖν of οὔκουν is for (Sm. §2953)—sc., that there would likely be doubt. Here, Thucydides argues that there should be no doubt. οὐκ εἰκός here means "it is not reasonable, not fair" (LSJ s.v. II) and takes three infinitives, sc., ἀπιστεῖν, σκοπεῖν, and νομίζειν. The negatives οὔκουν and οὐδέ do not negate the infinitives, for that would require μή (Sm. §2726), but they negate εἰκός, then the νομίζειν δέ shifts gears into a positive εἰκός. Hence, "therefore it is not reasonable to disbelieve . . . or to consider . . . , but it is reasonable to think that . . ."

λειπομένην δὲ τῶν νῦν. "but falling short of those now." LSJ s.v. λείπω B.II.3.

ἦν εἰκὸς κτλ. Here, εἰκός means "it is probable." Hence, "which [sc., the army] it is probable that Homer, being a poet, enhanced toward the greater [i.e., exaggerated]."

ἐνδεεστέρα. Understand τῶν νῦν.

10.4. τὰς μὲν . . . τὰς δέ. The article plus μὲν . . . δέ means "the one . . . the other," "some . . . some," or "the ones . . . the others." Here, the article serves as a pronoun. Sm. §1107. The partitive genitive χιλίων καὶ διακοσίων defines the group selected by the τὰς μὲν . . . τὰς δέ. Hence, "[Homer] makes some of the twelve hundred ships (those of the Boeotians) 120 men and others (those of Philoctetes) 50."

αὐτερέται indicates men who are both rowers and fighters at the same time. We get this definition from the lexicographer Pollux (1.95). Cf. Thuc. III.18.4, VI.91.4.

περίνεως. Accusative plural of an o-stem noun of the Attic declension. Sm. §§237–39. Nouns of the Attic declension originally had a long vowel before the stem-formative -o-, e.g., *περίνη⁻o⁻ς, which then underwent metathesis of quantity (Sm. §34) to become περίνεως. Note that the accent remains on the antepenult, as in the ancestral form. The accusative results from the development *περίνη⁻o⁻νς > *περίνε⁻ω⁻νς > περίνεως. The word means "a supernumerary or passenger."

οἱ ἐν τέλει. Technical term meaning "those in office." LSJ s.v. τέλος I.3.

ἄλλως τε καί. "especially, particularly." Sm. §2980.

10.5. τὸ μέσον σκοποῦντι. "to someone taking the average." The dative goes with φαίνεται.

ὡς. Here, "seeing that, given that" with the participle. Smyth does not seem to treat this use of ὡς. Cf. Thuc. II.65.11.

11.1. ἀπορίᾳ. Dative of cause or motive. Sm. §1517.

ὅσον refers to the army and is the object of βιοτεύσειν. πολεμοῦντα also modifies the army (not the leaders, in the plural) and means "while it is fighting."

ᾗ. Feminine dative relative pronoun used as a relative adverb meaning "for which reason, wherefore." It refers to the fact that the Greeks did not employ their whole force in battle. LSJ s.v. ᾗ II.2. This usage derives from the locative meanings of the dative. The combination ᾗ καί is used especially with a comparative (μᾶλλον) to mark the beginning of a clause emphasizing the consequences of what has just been said. Cf., e.g., Thuc. I.25.4, II.2.3, III.13.2, IV.1.3.

τοῖς αἰεὶ ὑπολειπομένοις ἀντίπαλοι ὄντες. "being a match for [the Greeks] who were left behind at any given time." αἰεί modifies ὑπολει-πομένοις, a present participle with imperfect force indicating repeated or customary action. Sm. §§1872a3, 1893.

11.2. εἷλον appears to lack an object (although it can easily be supplied), but the expectation of an object is maintained until it finally appears (τὴν Τροίαν) with the repetition of εἷλον at the end of the sentence.

διέφερον. Why is this not aorist in a past contrary-to-fact protasis parallel to ἦλθον? Because the imperfect in a contrary-to-fact protasis is contrary not only to a present reality but also to a continuous (ξυνέχως) reality in the past. Sm. §§2304, 2309b.

ἀντέχω. "hold out." In the active, this verb is generally intransitive, either absolute (i.e., without any complement) or with a dative of the party against which one holds out.

αὐτά γε δὴ ταῦτα. The combination γε δὴ means "a fortiori, particularly." Denniston Gr. Part.², 246 (5). Hence, "since all expeditions are weakened by lack of money, this very one especially [a fortiori] was so weakened."

διὰ τοὺς ποιητάς. "through the influence of the poets" (Warner); "under the tuition of the poets" (Crawley). Sm. §1685.2d. The preposition διά with the genitive expresses direct agency ("by") and with the accusative expresses indirect agency (fault, merit), i.e., "thanks to, by the aid of." LSJ s.v. B.III.1.

κατεσχηκότος. Genitive singular masculine perfect active participle of κατέχω. LSJ s.v. B.III. Here, it is intransitive, meaning "prevailing."

12.1. ἐπεὶ καί. Thucydides often uses this combination to introduce remarks that add to what has been said before and that can therefore seem obvious or natural. The punctuation in the Oxford text takes this clause as dependent on the preceding independent δηλοῦται clause. Other editors (e.g., Classen and Steup) take the ἐπεὶ καί as introducing an independent clause. Cf. Kühner-Gerth 2:461, §569a.1 Anmerkung 1: "The Greeks very frequently use ἐπεί where the causal clause does not form a subordinate part of the main clause, but rather ἐπεί has the force of γάρ in a main clause."

12.2. χρονία. Feminine adjective modifying ἀναχώρησις, meaning "tardy, late, after a long time."

ὥστε μὴ ἡσυχάσασαν αὐξηθῆναι. The negative μή applies to both the participle and the infinitive, doing double duty to negate each.

ἐνεόχμωσε. "made political innovations." This denominative omicron-contract verb based on the adjective νεοχμός, "new," usually occurs with a neuter plural noun or an adjective complement (πολλά). Chantraine (*Formation des noms*, §114) explains the adjective as νεο⁻ plus the "popular" expressive suffix ⁻χ⁻ plus the adjectival stem-formative ⁻μο⁻.

ὡς ἐπὶ πολύ. "for the most part." Cf. Thuc. II.13, ὡς ἐπὶ τὸ πολύ.

ἀφ' ὧν ἐκπίπτοντες τὰς πόλεις ἔκτιζον. "the exiles [those falling out] from which [sc., the cities] founded [new] cities." ἐκπίπτω is the *vox propria* for "be banished." LSJ s.v. 3.

12.3. ἀποδασμὸς ... ἀφ' ὧν ... "there was a portion [of the Boeotians] earlier in this land [Boeotia], part of whom also went on the expedition to Troy." ἀφ' ὧν refers to the collective ἀποδασμός, so the relative pronoun is plural. For ἀπό meaning "part of," see Sm. §1684. N and LSJ s.v. I.6.

12.4. ἔστιν ἅ. Fixed phrase meaning "some." Sm. §§2513–14.

13.1. τὰ πολλά. Adverbial, meaning "generally."

ἐπὶ ῥητοῖς γέρασι πατρικαὶ βασιλεῖαι. ἐπί with the dative expressing a condition, i.e., "on the basis of . . ." Sm. §1689.2c; LSJ s.v. ἐπί III.3, and s.v. ῥητός. Hence, "hereditary kingships with stated prerogatives."

ἐξηρτύετο. ἐξαρτύω means in the active "fit out" and in the transitive middle "fit out for oneself."

ἀντείχοντο. In the active, the verb ἀντέχω is generally intransitive and means "hold out." In the middle, it takes the genitive and means "hold onto, cling to."

13.4. ὧν ἴσμεν. Cf. 4.1.

13.5. αἰεὶ δή ποτε. "already from the earliest times, from of old."

τῶν Ἑλλήνων . . . ἐπιμισγόντων is the kernel of the genitive absolute, then τῶν Ἑλλήνων is modified with the appositives τῶν τε ἐντὸς . . . καὶ τῶν ἔξω. διὰ τῆς ἐκείνων [γῆς] is usually interpreted to mean "through their territory," i.e., through Corinthian territory. For the omission of γῆς, cf. Sm. §§1027b, 1302.

τοῖς παλαιοῖς ποιηταῖς. Dative of agent with the perfect middle used in a passive sense (δεδήλωται). Sm. §1488–90. The dative of agent (instead of ὑπό plus the genitive) is used with the perfect and pluperfect middle, with the verbal in ⁻τέος, and with verbal adjectives in ⁻τός.

κτησάμενοι refers to the Greeks, and παρέχοντες refers to the Corinthians. For this reason, some editors regard the κτησάμενοι phrase as a gloss, i.e., a marginal note that has worked its way into the text.

ἀμφότερα. Neuter plural (as the accent shows—the feminine would be ἀμφοτέρα with a long ultima) referring to ἐμπόριον in a *constructio ad sensum*. Sm. §926a. Hence, "providing a market, both kinds—sc., (1) by land through their isthmus between the Peloponnesus and the rest of Greece and (2) across their isthmus between the Corinthian Gulf and the Saronic Gulf. This is the natural interpretation, but Gomme (ad loc.) says that it means they had harbors on both gulfs. He notes, "Thucydides says nothing of Corinth being on an 'isthmic' route between the two seas—of sea traffic passing through her harbors between east and west." So, by his interpretation, "both kinds" mean "by land and by sea."

14.1. ἐξηρτυμένα. Perfect middle participle of ἐξαρτύω. Cf. 13.1.

ὥσπερ ἐκεῖνα. I.e., navies before the Trojan War.

14.3. ἀφ᾽ οὗ. "since." LSJ s.v. ἀπό II. Sm. §1684b.

διὰ πάσης [νεώς]. "over the whole ship, completely."

15.1. περιποιήσαντο. "acquire, gain possession of" (plus the accusative).

ὅμως. "nevertheless, still"; i.e., "despite what I have said, navies still . . ."

προσσχόντες. Intransitive thematic aorist of προσέχω. This verb is usually transitive, meaning "turn something toward something else" (e.g., προσέχω τὴν ναῦν [bring a ship to port] or προσέχω τὸν νοῦν [apply the mind]). But as an intransitive taking the dative, it means "devote oneself to, cultivate." LSJ s.v. 4b.

αὐτοῖς. Sc., τοῖς ναυτικοῖς.

ὅσοι μή. A relative clause in the indicative may be definite or indefinite. Sm. §§2505, 2509. If it is definite, it refers to some particular person, event, matter, etc. that is explicit. When it is indefinite, it refers to the sort of person, event, matter in general. Here, the relative clause is indefinite— referring to any and all who conquered islands, i.e., to the unexpressed subject of κατεστρέφοντο—and therefore takes the negative μή. Sm. §2506. If it had been definite, it would have taken the negative οὐ.

διαρκῆ. Accusative singular feminine of a two-ending s-stem adjective like ἀληθής. Sm. §292.

15.2. ὅθεν. Adverb in -θεν that serves as a substitute for ἐξ οὗ, the genitive of the relative, with πόλεμος as its antecedent. Sm. §§342, 2499.

ξυνέστη. Root aorist active used in a passive sense when referring to battle, meaning "was joined." LSJ s.v. συνίστημι II.1.

ἀπὸ τῆς ἐκείνων [γῆς]. Sm. §§1027b, 1302.

ἐπὶ καταστροφῇ. "for the purpose of subjection."

πολύ. "[not] much away from their own territory."

στρατείας ἐξῆσαν. Imperfect of ἔξειμι, "go out," which ought to be intransitive but here seems to take an accusative object. It is usually explained as a *cognate accusative* or an *internal object*. Sm. §§1563, 1567. Cf. ἐξῆλθον ἄλλας ὁδούς [They went forth on other journeys] (Xen. *Hell.* 1.2.17). Hence, here, "they did not go out on foreign expeditions."

οὐ γὰρ ξυνε, ιστήκεσαν πρὸς τὰς μεγίστας πόλεις ὑπήκοοι. "for they had not joined as subjects to the largest cities," i.e., in such alliances as the Delian League was to be. Crawley translates, "There was no union of subject cities around a great state."

ὡς ἕκαστοι. "each by themselves."

15.3. μάλιστα. "at the most." The only exception in this period was the Lelantine War between the Chalcidians and the Eretrians ca. 700 B.C. (date quite uncertain).

16.1. ἐπιγένετο δὲ ἄλλοις τε ἄλλοθι κωλύματα μὴ αὐξηθῆναι. ἐπιγίγνο-μαι means "happen in addition," with the implication of the unexpected or troublesome. LSJ s.v. II.1. τε goes with the following καί, making ἄλλοις and Ἴωσι quasi-parallel, but formally connecting ἐπιγένετο and ἐπεστρά-τευσε . . . καὶ . . . δούλωσε. Hence, "it happened to others and to the Ionians." Cf. 3.2. Yet Ἴωσι is formally dative after ἐπεστράτευσε and, at the same time, serves as a dative of interest with the genitive absolute προχωρησάντων κτλ. The adverb ἄλλοθι literally means "in another place" but here means "for other reasons." LSJ s.v. II. αὐξηθῆναι is an infinitive occurring with μή after an expression of hindering (κωλύματα). Sm. §§2038, 2744. Hence, "To several there occurred hindrances to in-crease, for various reasons, and to the Ionians [particularly] . . ."

17.1. τὸ ἐφ᾽ ἑαυτῶν. "their own interests." LSJ s.v. ἐπί A.I.2c.

αὔξειν. Articular infinitive with object, τὸν ἴδιον οἶκον.

δι᾽ ἀσφαλείας. διά with a noun in the genitive often serves as an adverb—hence, "safely." LSJ s.v. διά A.III.c. δι᾽ ἀσφαλείας ὅσον ἐδύναντο then means "as safely as they were able."

εἰ μὴ εἰ. Stuart Jones so reads. Many MSS (A, B, E, G, M) read only εἰ μή, and nowhere else in Thucydides do we find εἰ μὴ εἰ, though it does occur, e.g., at Pl. *Grg.* 480b. In any case, it means "except." LSJ s.v. εἰ VII.2a.

ἑκάστοις. Dative of agent with the unrepeated ἐπράχθη. Sm. §§1488, 1490.

οὕτω. This wraps up the arguments (τεκμήρια) why there were no large combined expeditions in the past.

κατείχετο. "was prevented, was held back." This verb takes the infinitive with μή after verbs of hindering. Sm. §2739.

18.1. The backbone of the sentence is ἐπειδὴ . . . τύραννοι . . . κατελύθησαν, . . . μάχη . . . ἐγένετο.

ἐπὶ πλεῖστον ὧν ἴσμεν χρόνον στασιάσασα. "although, for the longest time of all the [states] that we know, [Lacedaemon] was afflicted with faction . . ." The "faction" came to an end with the establishment of the Spartan constitution by Lycurgus, who brought εὐνομία to Sparta, more than four hundred years before the end of the Peloponnesian War.

δουλωσόμενος. Future participle of purpose with verb of motion. Sm. §2065.

οἵ τε ἀποστάντες . . . καὶ οἱ ξυμπολεμήσαντες refers to two categories of Greeks: (1) those who were Persian subjects and subsequently revolted and (2) those who were allied against the Persians.

18.3. διενεχθέντες. Aorist passive participle of διαφέρω, "be different," here meaning "being at variance, quarreling." LSJ s.v. διαφέρω IV.

εἴ τινές που διασταῖεν. This is not the protasis of a potential condition but, rather, the so-called iterative optative (Sm. §2340a), which is a transform into secondary sequence of an eventual conditional protasis— ἐάν plus the subjunctive. The combination εἴ . . . διασταῖεν, . . . ἐχώρουν forms a past general condition. διέστην, the intransitive root aorist of διΐστημι (LSJ s.v. II.2), here means "stand apart, be divided." Does it mean that they were in dispute with one another (Warner) or that they held off at first from the alliance and remained neutral (Crawley)? ἤδη means "eventually, by this time." LSJ s.v. So the sentence can mean "If any Greeks were ever at odds, by this time they were joining with one of the two sides" or "If ever any Greeks were holding off from the alliance, by this time they were joining one of the two sides."

ὥστε. "consequently." While ὥστε usually introduces result clauses (with finite verb) or result phrases (with infinitive), it sometimes introduces an independent coordinate clause. Sm. §2255.

τὰ μὲν . . . τὰ δὲ. Here, the neuter plural articles used as demonstratives are adverbial. Sm. §1111. Hence, "on the one hand . . . on the other . . ."

τὰς μελέτας ποιούμενοι. "getting practice." LSJ s.v. μελέτη II.1b.

19.1. φόρου. Genitive with ὑποτελεῖς, meaning "subject to tribute."

ὅπως πολιτεύσουσι θεραπεύοντες. θεραπεύω, basically meaning "serve, treat," here means "see to it that, take care that" (LSJ s.v. II.3) and is therefore a verb of effort that takes ὅπως plus the future. Sm. §§2209–11.

Ἀθηναῖοι δὲ κτλ. The verb ἡγοῦντο, used absolutely here, serves for both subjects—sc., the Lacedaemonians and the Athenians—and the participles specify the manner in which each led their respective leagues.

τάξαντες φέρειν. τάσσω basically means "place in order" but here means "assess (a tribute or tax)." LSJ s.v. III.3. φέρειν, the *vox propria* for taxes, means "to pay" and is here most likely after τάσσω analogously with infinitives after verbs of will and desire. Sm. §§1991–94. Alternatively, it is an epexegetical infinitive, as in "money to pay."

ἀκραιφνοῦς is in predicative position, implying a temporal effect. Hence, "with the alliance when it was intact."

20.1. μὲν οὖν marks a transition in the argument from the narrative to the discussion about the reliability of tradition. "Often the μέν clause sums up and rounds off the old topic, while the δέ clause introduces the new one" (Denniston, *Gr. Part.*², 472). But here, instead of the expected δέ, the new topic is introduced by the χαλεπὰ ὄντα phrase and the γάρ following.

πιστεῦσαι. Epexegetical infinitive, i.e., an infinitive used as an accusative of respect with the adjective χαλεπά. Hence, "difficult with respect to trusting."

ἑξῆς. Adverb in attributive position, here meaning "one by one."

20.2. γοῦν. "for example." "γοῦν commonly confirms a previous general assertion by giving a special instance of its truth" (Sm. §2830).

τι. Subject of μεμηνῦσθαι.

ἐκ τῶν ξυνειδότων. Rare use of ἐκ with genitive to mark the agent, instead of the usual ὑπό. Sm. §1688c.

ὡς προειδότος. "This particle [ὡς] sets forth the ground of belief on which the agent acts, and denotes the thought, assertion, real or presumed intention, in the mind of the subject of the principal verb or of some other person mentioned prominently in the sentence without implicating the speaker or writer" (Sm. §2086).

20.3. μιᾷ ψήφῳ προστίθεσθαι ἑκάτερον. "each assent with one vote." This is the true case, the erroneous belief being that they have two votes each. LSJ s.v. προστίθημι B.3.

ἀταλαίπωρος. "not painstaking." This feminine adjective modifies ζήτησις. Compound adjectives have two endings. Sm. §288.

21.1. ἐκ δὲ τῶν εἰρημένων . . . ἀποχρώντως. The backbone of this sentence follows.

οὐκ ἁμαρτάνοι ἄν
  (1) τις νομίζων τοιαῦτα
    ἃ διῆλθον
  (2) καὶ οὔτε πιστεύων
    ὡς ὑμνήκασι
    οὔτε ὡς ξυνέθησαν (αὐτὰ)
      ὄντα ἀνεξέλεγκτα
      καὶ ἐκνενικηκότα
  (3) ἡγησάμενος δέ (ἃ διῆλθον) ηὑρῆσθαι

τοιαῦτα is predicative after νομίζων—hence, "thinking what I say to be such." It refers to what has gone before, sc., the result of patient research for the truth.

ἐπὶ τὸ προαγωγότερον τῇ ἀκροάσει ἢ ἀληθέστερον. When two adjectives are compared with one another (as in "more attractive to hear than true"), both are put into the comparative degree. Sm. §1080. ἐπὶ makes the expression adverbial, as in ἐπὶ πλέον, "mostly." Kühner-Gerth 1:505, §438.III.3b. Hence, "in a manner more attractive to hear than true."

ὡς παλαιὰ εἶναι ἀποχρώντως. Absolute infinitive. Sm. §2012c.

A translation of this difficult sentence (the difficulty of which can be seen by comparing how widely the translators differ) follows.

> From the stated evidences, nevertheless, someone would not go wrong by considering what I have recounted to be very much of that kind [i.e., reliable]; not, rather, believing as the poets have sung with decorated exaggeration concerning these matters or as the chroniclers, in a manner more attractive to hear than true, have composed things that are incapable of being disproved and things that have— many of them in time—won their way into the fabulous in a way that cannot be believed [ἀπίστως]; but (one would not go wrong) considering [what I have recounted] to have been researched from the clearest evidences, given that the matters are sufficiently ancient.

21.2. καίπερ τῶν ἀνθρώπων κτλ. Concessive expression with the participle in the genitive absolute. Sm. §2083. Hence, "although."

ὡς παλαιὰ εἶναι. Absolute infinitive. Sm. §2012. Hence, "considering their antiquity."

παυσαμένων . . . θαυμαζόντων. θαυμαζόντων is not, as one might think, a supplementary participle with παύομαι but a third genitive absolute participle parallel to κρινόντων and παυσαμένων. There is no connective to separate θαυμαζόντων, a case of asyndeton. How do we know this without an explicit signal? First, the logic of the argument makes it necessary, since the point is overestimating the importance of the past. Second, μᾶλλον functions as a contrasting element, which serves to indicate the parataxis. Hence, "while men always judge the current war in which they are fighting to be the greatest but have a great wonder for the past when they have stopped [fighting], this war will stand out . . ."

δηλώσει . . . γεγενημένος is a species of indirect discourse. Like verbs of perception (Sm. §2110ff.), verbs of knowing and showing take the accusative and an accusative participle. E.g., τοῦτο τοίνυν τὸ γράμμα παντελῶς δηλοῖ ψευδῆ τὴν διαθήκην οὖσαν [This clause now shows completely that the will was forged] (Dem. 45.34). (Sm. §2106) But when the subject of the verb of showing is the same as the subject of the participle, it is not repeated, and the participle is in the nominative. Hence, "Yet this war [itself] will stand out to anyone drawing conclusions from the facts themselves as greater than those [that preceded it]."

22.1. ὅσα. The antecedent is the following λεχθέντων.

ὡς δ' ἂν ἐδόκουν . . . εἰπεῖν. ἂν goes with εἰπεῖν, which represents an independent potential optative (Sm. §§1845, 1848) downgraded to an infinitive phrase. Here, ἐδόκουν is personal rather than impersonal. Sm. §1983. Hence, "as it [literally, "they"] seemed to me they would have said what is most appropriate under the current circumstances."

ἐχομένῳ. "[me] maintaining" (plus the genitive γνώμης) LSJ s.v. ἔχω C.I.1.

ὅτι ἐγγύτατα. "as closely as possible."

οὕτως εἴρηται. This οὕτως in the main clause is the hook on which hangs the ὡς that introduces the subordinate clause at the beginning of the sentence.

22.2. ἐκ τοῦ παρατυχόντος. "from any Tom, Dick, or Harry"—literally, "one who chanced to be by."

οὐ πυνθανόμενος . . . ἀλλὰ . . . ἐπεξέλθων. ἐπεξέρχομαι means "discuss, relate, or examine accurately and fully." LSJ s.v. II.3. Here, it refers not to the narrative but to the investigation—hence, "examine."

οἷς. The referent of this relative is πραχθέντων, but it is not the antecedent. The relative clause is nominal, and the antecedent is omitted (Sm. §2509); i.e., the whole relative clause is the object of ἐπεξέλθων. τε . . . καὶ marks the parallel constructions οἷς αὐτὸς παρῆν and (ἃ) παρὰ τῶν ἄλλων (ἀπηγγέλθη). παρὰ τῶν ἄλλων is elliptical, but the ideas can be filled out by the parallelism with the discussion of τὰ λεχθέντα at the beginning of the paragraph.

A translation of the sentence follows.

> I deemed it worthy to write neither the facts of actions in the war that I picked up from any old source nor even as it seemed to me, but by investigating both events at which I was present and events reported to me by others, with as much accuracy as possible.

22.3. ὡς . . . ἔχοι. ἔχω plus the genitive means "to be well off for something, to excel at something." LSJ s.v. B.II.2b. Hence, here, "according as anyone excelled at goodwill for one of the two sides or memory." This is a comparative adverbial clause with the optative in secondary sequence (after ἔλεγον) indicating undefined frequency, sometimes called the *iterative optative*. Kühner-Gerth 2:491, §580.I.2. Cf. ξυνετίθεσαν . . . ὡς ἕκαστόν τι ξυμβαίνοι [they arranged [the stones] according as each fit] (Thuc. IV.4.2). It is akin to general protases (present general and past general) and general relative clauses. In primary sequence, the clause would have had ὡς ἄν plus the subjunctive.

22.4. τὸ μὴ μυθῶδες αὐτῶν. The negative μή is here generalizing meaning "whatever is not romantic" (Sm. §2735), and αὐτῶν is partitive, referring to Thucydides' history. Hence, "whatever of these pages is not romantic."

ὅσοι δὲ . . . ἕξει. The backbone of this sentence follows.

ἕξει [it will be possible]
   (τούτους) κρίνειν αὐτὰ ὠφέλιμα
   ὅσοι βουλήσονται σκοπεῖν
     τὸ σαφὲς
      τῶν τε γενομένων
      καὶ τῶν μελλόντων

The ὅσοι βουλήσονται clause serves as the accusative subject of the complementary infinitive κρίνειν, which takes a double accusative. Sm. §1613.

αὐτά refers to the history, as it does earlier in the sentence.

τῶν μελλόντων ποτὲ αὖθις κατὰ τὸ ἀνθρώπινον τοιούτων καὶ παραπλησίων ἔσεσθαι. "things that will someday be again like these or very nearly like these in accordance with what is human."

ἀρκούντως ἕξει. "it will be enough." Sm. §1438.

ξυγκεῖται serves as the passive of ξυντίθημι, "compose." LSJ s.v. συντίθημι II.3, s.v. συγκεῖμαι II.2.

23.1. μῆκος τε μέγα προύβη. μέγα is predicative. Hence, "the length went on [to become] long."

ξυνηνέχθη. Aorist passive of συμφέρω, "happen." LSJ s.v. B.III.2. Here, it is used impersonally, with παθήματα as the accusative subject of γενέσθαι. Hence, "It happened that there were sufferings . . ." Strictly speaking, the infinitive phrase is the subject of ξυνηνέχθη.

οἷα οὐχ ἕτερα. Formula meaning "unprecedented." Literally, "such as there were not others."

23.3. σπανιώτερον. Neuter comparative of the adjective used as the comparative of the adverb. Sm. §345.

οὐκ ἄπιστα κατέστη. "became credible."

ἐπέσχον. The accent of finite verbs never recedes beyond the augment. Sm. §426. Here, the verb is intransitive, meaning "prevail, predominate, spread." LSJ s.v. ἐπέχω VI.2.

ἰσχυρότατοι is predicative. Hence, "and they were very strong."

παρά. "compared with" (plus the accusative). Sm. §1692.3c; LSJ s.v. C.I.7.

ἔστι παρ' οἷς. "among some." ἔστιν οἷς is the dative plural of the fixed phrase εἰσὶν οἵ, "some." Sm. §2514. Whenever this fixed formula is used with a preposition, the preposition goes in the middle. Cf. Thuc. V.25.2, ἔστιν ἐν οἷς.

ἅμα ξυνεπέθετο. "joined in attacking all at once." LSJ s.v. συνεπιτίθημι II.1.

23.4. αὐτοῦ. Sc., τοῦ πολέμου; genitive after ἄρχομαι. Sm. §1348. Smyth (Sm. §1734.5) says that the active ἄρχω contrasts one beginner of an action with another; i.e., it indicates that someone begins before someone else. E.g., ἄρχειν πολέμου would mean "strike the first blow of the war." But the middle ἄρχομαι means "make one's own beginning," contrasting not with someone else but with the later stages of an action. LSJ s.v. I.

23.5. διότι ἔλυσαν. Implied indirect question after "causes and differences." LSJ s.v. διότι I.2.

τοῦ μή τινα ζητῆσαί ποτε. Genitive articular infinitive of purpose. Sm. §§1408, 2032e. The verb ζητέω usually means "seek, ask" but may mean "feel the need to seek or ask," as here. LSJ s.v. III. Cf. Hdt. 1.94.

23.6. αἵδ'. I.e., "as follows." The stated causes are those that Thucydides will presently narrate, namely, the affair of Epidamnus and the affair of

Potidaea. In the historical writers, ὅδε especially indicates what is immediately to come in the narrative. LSJ s.v. II.2.

ἀφ᾽ ὧν. "as a result of which." LSJ s.v. ἀπό III.6. Sm. §1684.1.c3.

24.5. To keep the subjects straight throughout this passage, bear in mind that δέ serves to change from one subject to another. One party is the δῆμος, also called here οἱ ἐν τῇ πόλει, i.e., the democratic party. The other party is οἱ δύνατοι, or the oligarchical party.

οἱ δὲ ἐπελθόντες. οἱ δέ means the oligarchs, the δύνατοι.

24.6. οἱ δὲ changes the subject to the democrats.

τούς τε φεύγοντας ξυναλλάξαι σφισί. "to reconcile the exiles [the ousted oligarchs] to them [the democrats]."

25.1. ἐν ἀπόρῳ εἴχοντο θέσθαι τὸ παρόν. "they were at a loss how to handle the present [circumstance]." ἔχομαι is virtually a substitute for the verb "to be." Cf. Thuc. III.22.6, ἐν ἀπόρῳ εἶναι. This meaning of ἔχομαι was oddly left out of the first printing of LSJ, but it is in the supplement to LSJ s.v. ἔχω C.V ("stand or be"). See LSJ s.v. τίθημι VII.1.Med.

εἰ παραδοῖεν . . . καὶ . . . πειρῷντο. Indirect yes-no question in secondary sequence with optional optative. Sm. §§2638, 2671, 2677. The original direct question would have been a deliberative subjunctive: παραδῶμεν . . . πειρώμεθα Sm. §§1805–8, ("whether we should hand over the city . . . and try . . .").

τιμωρίαν τινὰ . . . ἀπ᾽ αὐτῶν ποιεῖσθαι. "to obtain some assistance from them [the Corinthians]." LSJ s.v. τιμωρία II ("succour") s.v. ποιέω A.II.2.Med. ("procure for oneself, gain").

ὁ δ᾽ αὐτοῖς ἀνεῖλε. ὁ δέ is Apollo, and ἀναιρέω is the *vox propria* for giving an oracular response. LSJ s.v. III.

25.3. μίσει. Dative singular of the s-stem noun τὸ μῖσος.

25.4. Κορινθίῳ ἀνδρὶ προκαταρχόμενοι τῶν ἱερῶν. "bestow the first portion of the sacrifices on a Corinthian."

ὁμοῖα. Neuter plural used as an adverb. LSJ s.v. ὅμοιος (or ὁμοῖος) C.I.

προύχειν ἔστιν ὅτε ἐπαιρόμενοι. "boasting sometimes that they excelled." Sm. §2515 (ἔστιν ὅτε); LSJ s.v. ἐπαίρω II.1 ad fin.

κλέος ἐχόντων τὰ περὶ τὰς ναῦς. The genitive participle modifies Φαιάκων. The Phaeacians "had naval affairs as their *kleos* or source of renown."

ᾗ καὶ μᾶλλον. The feminine dative relative pronoun ᾗ is here used as a relative adverb meaning "for which reason, wherefore" and refers to the ground of the Corcyrean claims. LSJ s.v. ᾗ II.2. This usage derives from the locative meanings of the dative. The combination ᾗ καί is used especially with a comparative (μᾶλλον) to mark the beginning of a clause emphasizing the consequences of what has just been said. Cf. 11.1.

ὑπῆρχον. ὑπάρχω often serves as a substitute for "to be." LSJ s.v. B.4.

26.1. οἰκήτορά τε τὸν βουλόμενον ἰέναι κελεύοντες. "inviting anyone who wishes to go as a settler."

φρουρούς is grammatically construed with κελεύοντες ἰέναι but semantically more dependent on ἔπεμπον.

26.2. δέει. Dative singular of τὸ δέος followed by a clause of fearing.

26.3. κατ᾽ ἐπήρειαν modifies ἐκέλευον adverbially, meaning "brusquely, haughtily, threateningly."

τοὺς φεύγοντας is the object of δέχεσθαι and refers to the banished aristocrats.

27.1. ἐπὶ τῇ ἴσῃ καὶ ὁμοίᾳ. I.e., on the condition of equal status with the original colonists. The missing dative noun would be δίκῃ. LSJ s.v. ἴσος II.2.

27.2. εἰ ἄρα κωλύοιντο is not really a condition but an "in case" clause (Sm. §2354) with optative in secondary sequence. The asking is not causally dependent on the preventing, as in a true condition (e.g., "If they prevent . . . , then they ask."); rather, they ask in case there will be prevention.

28.1. ὡς οὐ μετὸν αὐτοῖς Ἐπιδάμνου. μετὸν is an impersonal neuter accusative absolute participle with ὡς. Sm. §2076. ὡς indicates that this is what the Corcyreans asserted. Sm. §2086.

28.2. δίκας δοῦναι. This construction usually means "pay a penalty" but here means "submit to arbitration." LSJ s.v. δίκη IV.3.

τούτους κρατεῖν. The infinitive phrase goes with the earlier ἤθελον, and the τούτους refers to ὁποτέρων. Hence, "they were willing that those should have control [of the colony]."

28.3. εἴων. The verb ἐάω usually means "allow," but here, with a negative οὐκ, it means "persuade not to, advise against" and takes the infinitive. LSJ s.v. 2. Cf. Thuc. I.133.

28.4. βουλεύσεσθαι. In the middle, βουλεύω means "think about it."

αὑτούς. I.e., the Corinthians.

28.5. Καὶ ὥστε. "under the condition that." LSJ s.v. B.I.4.

29.1. προεροῦντα. Future participle of purpose with verb of motion. Sm. §2065.

ἄραντες. Intransitive aorist participle of ἀείρω, "get under sail." LSJ s.v. I.5.

29.3. ζεύξαντες τὰς παλαιάς. "having reinforced the older ships." This means either fitting crossbeams from one side of the ship to the other (as explained by Gregory of Corinth, a grammarian of the twelfth century A.D.) or, possibly, fastening cables around the ship—or both.

29.5. αὑτοῖς ξυνέβη. "it happened to them," i.e., the Corcyreans as a whole, both those on sea and those besieging Epidamnus.

παραστήσασθαι. "caused it [Epidamnus] to come to terms." LSJ s.v. C.II.1. The subject is τοὺς πολιορκοῦντας, i.e., the Corcyreans. Ἐπίδαμνον is the object of the participle πολιορκοῦντας and, by brachylogy (Sm. §3018k), of παραστήσασθαι.

ὥστε. "under the condition that." LSJ s.v. B.I.4.

ἐπήλυτδας ἀποδόσθαι. I.e., they would sell the foreigners as slaves. In the middle, ἀποδίδωμι means "sell." LSJ s.v. III.

δήσαντας ἔχειν. "keep the Corinthians by binding them," i.e., keep them prisoner. δήσαντας here agrees with the unexpressed subject of the infinitive and does not refer to the Corinthians.

30.2. τῆς γῆς. Partitive genitive with τέμνειν. Hence, "to waste parts of the land." LSJ s.v. IV.3; Sm. §1341.

τὸ ἐπίνειον. "harbor."

31.2. ὡς τοὺς Ἀθηναίους. Here, ὡς is a preposition taking the accusative. Sm. §1702.

31.3. καὶ τὸ αὐτῶν προσγενόμενον. αὐτῶν refers to the Athenians. Hence, "lest the Athenian navy added to the Corcyrean be an impediment."

θέσθαι. After the noun ἐμπόδιον [impediment], which is analogous to a verb of hindering (without redundant μή). Sm. §2744.7. Cf. οὐ κωλύει τοῦτο ποιεῖν, meaning "nothing hinders doing this." Hence, "lest [the combined navies] be an impediment to their managing [θέσθαι] the war in the way they want."

32.1. προὐφειλομένης. Προοφείλω generally means "owe beforehand" and here means "owed as a long-standing debt."

ξύμφορα δέονται. Usually, δέομαι takes a genitive, but if the object is a neuter adjective or pronoun, it will be accusative. LSJ s.v. II.2; Sm. §1398.

τὴν χάριν βέβαιον ἕξουσι. "they will keep their gratitude firm." The position of the article shows that βέβαιον is predicative. Sm. §1168. In Thucydides and Plato, βέβαιος is always a two-ending adjective.

32.3. For τυγχάνω without a supplementary participle, see Sm. §2119. Construe ἡμῖν with τετύχηκε—hence, "it has turned out for us [to be] . . ."

τὸ αὐτὸ ἐπιτήδευμα. "The same old policy" is at once (a) unreasonable from your standpoint and (b) not in our interest.

πρός and ἐς mean the same thing, "regarding, with respect to." Thucydides alternates these prepositions often (cf., e.g., I.38.1, III.37.2). πρός ὑμᾶς [with respect to you] and ἐς τὰ ἡμέτερα [with respect to our interests] are parallel. ἐς τὴν χρείαν means "in the matter of [our] request."

32.4. τῇ τοῦ πέλας γνώμῃ. Dative with the preverb ξυν⁻. Hence, "the policy of a neighbor."

32.5. τὴν ναυμαχίαν . . . Κορινθίους. The two accusatives can be explained by analogy with such expressions as νικᾶν τινα ναυμαχίαν, which means "beat somebody in a sea battle." Cf. Thuc. VII.66.2.

The nouns κίνδυνος, ἀνάγκη, and συγγνώμη function without the expected ἔσται or ἐστί. Sm. §944.

εἰ ἐσόμεθα ὑπ' αὐτοῖς. Real condition with future protasis. Sm. §2328. The apodosis would be κίνδυνος ἔσται. This embodies a threat or warning (minatory-monitory condition). ὑπ' αὐτοῖς means "under their power."

εἰ μὴ μετὰ . . . τολμῶμεν. μή negates only μετὰ κακίας—not the whole clause (cf. Thuc. I.37.1, III.14.1)—and generalizes the expression (hence, "not from any sinister motive"). Sm. §2735. τολμῶμεν is indicative in a causal "if" clause dependent on συγγνώμη. Sm. §2247. ἐνάντια is the neuter plural object of τολμῶμεν, which here has the meaning "venture on a policy opposite."

33.1. κατὰ πολλά. "in many respects"—specifically, the three reasons introduced respectively by πρῶτον, ἔπειτα, and τε.

ὡς ἂν μάλιστα. ὡς μάλιστα means "certainly." Here, ἂν stands in a fixed phrase without a verb (Sm. §1766b), which can be supplied from context (e.g., ὡς ἂν μάλιστα γένοιτο).

33.2. Τίς εὐπραξία . . . ἰσχύν. The backbone of this sentence follows.

> Τίς εὐπραξία σπανιωτέρα (ἐστίν)
> ἢ τίς τοῖς πολεμίοις λυπηροτέρα
>   εἰ δύναμις πάρεστιν
>   ἣν ἂν ὑμῖν προσγενέσθαι ἐτιμήσασθε
>   διδοῦσα ἑαυτήν
>   καὶ φέρουσα
>   ἀρετήν
>   χάριν
>   ἰσχύν

ἐς τοὺς πολλοὺς ἀρέτην. "virtue in the eyes of the world" (the usual meaning of this phrase).

οἷς δὲ ἐπαμυνεῖτε χάριν. "gratitude of those whom you will defend." If this phrase were filled out, it would be χάριν τούτων οἷς δὲ ἐπαμυνεῖτε.

καὶ ὀλίγοι . . . παραγίγνονται. The backbone of this sentence follows.

ὀλίγοι . . . παραγίγνονται
   δεόμενοι συμμαχίας
   διδόντες οὐχ ἧσσον ἀσφάλειαν . . .
   ἢ ληψόμενοι
     (τούτοις οὓς) > οἷς ἐπικαλοῦνται

The relative clause οἷς ἐπικαλοῦνται is the indirect object of διδόντες with incorporated antecedent (Sm. §§2536, 2538). In the middle, ἐπικαλοῦμαι means "call someone to one's aid."

33.3. αἰσθάνεται, being a verb of perception, takes an accusative plus a participle as the form of indirect discourse. Sm. §§2110–11.

φόβῳ τῷ ὑμετέρῳ. For the use of the pronominal adjective for the objective genitive, see Sm. §§1331, 1334.

πολεμησείοντας. The verb πολεμησείω is a desiderative of πολεμέω. Sm. §868; Schwyzer, 798.

δυναμένους παρ' αὐτοῖς. "having powerful influence with them [the Spartans]."

προκαταλαμβάνοντας ἡμᾶς νῦν ἐς τὴν ὑμετέρην ἐπιχείρησιν. "overpowering us first in anticipation of an attempt on you." The pronominal adjective is used for the objective genitive. Sm. §§1331, 1334.

μηδὲ δυοῖν φθάσθαι ἁμάρτωσιν. μηδὲ continues the negative purpose clause with the subjunctive ἁμάρτωσιν. The verb ἁμαρτάνω, "miss, fail to," here takes the genitive δυοῖν (LSJ s.v. I.4)—hence, "fail at two things." Gomme (ad loc.) says the two things are (1) to harm the Corcyreans and (2) to increase Corinth's own security. φθάσθαι is the root aorist middle infinitive of the verb φθάνω, meaning "to get there first, anticipate, be quick." Some would argue that δυοῖν is a dative of respect, that ἁμαρτάνω takes the infinitive φθάσθαι, and that the entire phrase means "lest they fail to be first with respect to two things." Βυτ ἁμαρτάνω ordinarily takes not an infinitive (as in "to fail to do something") but, rather, a participle. LSJ s.v. ἁμαρτάνω II.1. So φθάσθαι is here an infinitive functioning like an accusative of respect, and the phrase means "lest they fail in two aims with respect to being first." The editors have striven mightily over this φθάσθαι, and some argue that it is an inserted gloss and thus does not belong there.

33.4. ἡμέτερόν (ἐστι). "It is our job to . . ." By a construction according to sense, the neuter possessive pronoun is picked up by the genitive plurals διδόντων and δεξαμένων.

34.1. μαθόντων. Third plural aorist active imperative.

ἐπὶ τῷ δοῦλοι . . . εἶναι. "on the condition of being slaves." LSJ s.v. ἐπί B.III.3; Sm. §1689.2c. The subject of the articular infinitive is nominative instead of accusative "when the infinitive, expressing some action or state of the subject of the main verb, has the article in an oblique case" (Sm. §1973a).

34.2. μετελθεῖν. "prosecute, pursue" a matter. LSJ s.v. μετέρχομαι IV.3.

34.3. δεομένοις τε ἐκ τοῦ εὐθέος μὴ ὑπουργεῖν. "nor render help [to the Corinthians] when they ask directly." Cf. LSJ s.v. εὐθύς A2. ἐκ τοῦ εὐθέος could go adverbially with either δεομένοις or ὑπουργεῖν.

ὁ γὰρ ἐλαχίστας . . . διατελοίη. "That one who makes fewest his regrets for doing a favor to enemies would turn out safest." ἐλαχίστας is in predicative position, so λαμβάνων is factitive. Cf. Thuc. II.43.2.

35.1. μηδετέρων. Here we have "μηδετέρων instead of οὐδετέρων because, although this relationship is actual, the hypothetical character of the participle δεχόμενοι influences its object" (Classen and Steup, ad loc.); i.e., δεχόμενοι is here tantamount to a conditional clause, as if the text were ἐὰν ἡμᾶς δέχησθε, οὐ λύσετε, an eventual condition with future apodosis, or future-more-vivid condition. This then influences any negative dependent on the participle and requires the negative μή of an "if" clause. Sm. §2728.

35.3. καὶ δεινὸν εἰ . . . Real condition with future indicative in the protasis, indicating a threat or warning. This is Smyth's "emotional future condition" (Sm. §§2297, 2328), sometimes called a minatory-monitory condition.

θήσονται. "they will consider you in the wrong if you are persuaded." The "if" must be understood from the genitive absolute, which substitutes for a conditional. An object, ὑμᾶς, is understood from the ὑμῶν of the genitive absolute. Cf. LSJ s.v. ἀδίκημα I.1, s.v. τίθημι B.II.3 ("consider").

35.4. οὐκ ὅπως . . . ἀλλὰ καί. "not only not [so far from] . . . but also." Sm. §2763b. Hence, "you will not only fail to be preventers of your enemies, but you will also allow them to increase their strength." περιοράω means "overlook" and then "allow." LSJ s.v. II.2.

ἣν οὐ δίκαιον. The antecedent of ἣν is δύναμιν in the preceding sentence, and another προσλαβεῖν is to be understood. Hence, "to increase which power is not just." What is just follows. There is a reversal of meaning with ἀλλ᾿, and δίκαιον is used positively for the rest of the sentence; its subjects are the infinitives κωλύειν, πέμπειν, and βοηθεῖν, things that are just.

κἀκείνων κωλύειν τοὺς ἐκ τῆς ὑμετέρας μισθοφόρους. "prevent their mercenaries [to be taken] from your strength." ἐκείνων is possessive and refers to the Corinthians. κωλύειν with accusative but no infinitive is rare, and perhaps προσλαβέσθαι is to be understood. Classen and Steup (ad loc.) say this is an unusual variation for the expression κἀκείνους ἐρέτας μισθοῦσθαι, meaning "prevent (them) from hiring oarsmen." With ἐκ τῆς ὑμετέρας, understand ἀρχῆς.

ἀπὸ τοῦ προφανοῦς is tantamount to an adverb, meaning "openly."

35.5. καὶ ναυτικῆς . . . διδομένης, οὐκ ὁμοῖα ἡ ἀλλοτρίωσις. "Since the alliance being offered is naval and not a land alliance, a rejection is not the same [as it would be for merely a land alliance]."

ἐᾶν and ἔχειν must be understood as imperatives. This is rare in prose, where it is supposed to have "a solemn or formal force" (Sm. §2013).

36.1. This is a lollapalooza of a sentence and will repay careful study. Although it is very complicated, it has only one main verb, the third singular aorist active imperative γνώτω. The subjects of this imperative are the ὅτῳ . . . λέγεσθαι clause and the (ὅς) φοβεῖται clause (whose relative is implied by the preceding ὅτῳ).

The indirect statement constructions after γνώτω are participial after a verb of knowing. Sm. §2106. Further, when the participle applies to the subject of the verb of perceiving, as with βουλευόμενος and προνοῶν, it will be in the nominative instead of the accusative. Unfortunately, Smyth does not make this point clear, but it can be gleaned from his examples in Sm. §2106. Four constructions follow γνώτω.

1. τὸ δεδιὸς . . . φοβῆσον [that his fear frightens your enemies]
2. τὸ θαρσοῦν . . . ἐσόμενον [that your boldness will be weaker]
3. οὐ βουλευόμενος [that he is not making a decision about . . .]
4. οὐ προνοῶν [that he is not making provision for . . .]

The ὅταν clause follows upon οὐ προνοῶν—hence, "he is not making provision . . . whenever he hesitates." ἐνδοιάζῃ takes the complementary infinitive προσλαβεῖν—hence, "hesitates to attach a country to his side that . . ."

Next, consider the circumstantial participles ἰσχὺν ἔχον and ἀσθενὲς ὄν. Thucydides is playing with the ironic contrasts between strength and weakness: what is weak seems strong and what is strong seems weak. This is crossed with the contrast between fear and boldness. The participles ἔχον and ὄν modify the two substantivized neuter participles τὸ δεδιός and τὸ θαρσοῦν. Thucydides likes to use a neuter participle instead of the corresponding abstract noun (e.g., τὸ δέος and τὸ θάρσος): this is known as the schema Thucydideum. The circumstantial participles can be regarded as causal. Hence, "His fear, because it has power, frightens the enemies more. . . . But if he does not accept us as allies, boldness, because it is weak, will be more deficient in the eyes of enemies, who are growing strong."

μὴ δεξαμένου (ἡμᾶς). This is probably not a genitive absolute but a possessive genitive parallel to αὐτοῦ—hence, "the boldness of the man who has not received us as allies"—but the implication is that his boldness is weak because he has not received the allies.

δι' αὐτὰ [sc., ξυμφέροντα] πειθόμενος. "although persuaded by virtue of these advantages." Sm. §1685.2b. The concessive force of the circumstantial participle (Sm. §2066) arises out of the logic of the sentence.

αὐταῖς refers to τῶν Ἀθηνῶν [Athens]. Notice that it is not Ἀθηναίων.

ὅσον οὐ παρόντα. The fixed phrase ὅσον οὐ means "almost, all but," referring to time. Sm. §2766; cf. Thuc. II.94.1.

τὸ αὐτίκα περισκοπῶν. "restricting his vision to the immediate situation." ἐς . . . πόλεμον goes with προσλαβεῖν; hence, "restricting his vision to the immediate situation, he hesitates for the war that is to come—indeed, is almost here—to attach to his side a country . . ."

οἰκειοῦταί τε καὶ πολεμοῦται. "be made a friend [οἰκεῖος] and an enemy [i.e., or an enemy]." Whether Corcyra is a friend or an enemy, the consequences will be very great. For τε καὶ used for alternatives, see Sm. §2976.

A more or less literal (and clumsy, but syntactically revealing) translation of the sentence follows.

> To whomever it seems that these things are spoken as advantages but who fears lest, if he is persuaded by virtue of these advantages, he break the truce, let him understand that his fear, since it has strength, is more frightening to his enemies, but if he does not accept us as allies, his boldness will be more deficient in the eyes of his strong enemies; and [let him understand further] that he is deciding, at the same time, not more now concerning Corcyra than [concerning] Athens; and that he is not looking toward the greatest advantages for her [Athens] whenever, because he is looking only at the immediate situation, he hesitates to attach to himself, for the war that is going to come and is as good as present, a country that is made a friend or an enemy with the greatest consequences.

36.2. τῆς τε γὰρ Ἰταλίας καὶ Σικελίας καλῶς παράπλου κεῖται. "[Corcyra] is beautifully situated for the sailing route to Italy and Sicily." The expression καλῶς κεῖται [is beautifully situated] is analogous to the use of ἔχω with an adverb (Sm. §1438), and παράπλου is a case of the genitive with adverbs (Sm. §1441). The genitive is used with adverbs of quality or manner (εὖ, καλῶς, ὁμοίως, and several others) in connection with intransitive verbs (ἔχειν, εἶναι, and κεῖσθαι) to indicate what the adverb applies to. Cf. Kühner-Gerth 1:382, §419.1. Cf. Thuc. III.92.4: τοῦ πολέμου καλῶς ἐδόκει ἡ πόλις καθίστασθαι . . . τῆς τε ἐπὶ Θρᾴκης παρόδου χρησίμως ἕξειν [they thought that the city was well situated for the war and would prove useful for the march along Thrace] (Smyth's translation, Sm. §1441).

ἐκεῖθεν. "from that place," i.e., from Sicily to the Peloponnesians.

τὸ ἐνθένδε ναυτικόν with the adverb in attributive position means "the fleet from here," i.e., from the Peloponnesus.

πρὸς τἀκεῖ. "to the things [events] there [Sicily and Italy]."

ἐπελθεῖν and παραπέμψαι are dependent on οὐκ ἐᾶν—hence, "to prevent the reinforcing and the sending." Sm. §2692. But οὐκ ἐᾶν becomes μὴ ἐᾶν because of the ὥστε. Sm. §2759a.

36.3. The backbone of this sentence is μάθοιτε ἂν μὴ προέσθαι ἡμᾶς τῷδε. The ἄν is repeated: the first ἄν lets the reader know a potential is on its way, and the second marks the potential itself. Sm. §1765. τῷδε, meaning "by means of this following thing," stands for the whole of the next sentence down to the end of the speech. τῷδε is defined by βραχυτάτῳ κεφαλαίῳ—hence, "by means of the very brief summary that follows." τοῖς τε ξύμπασι καὶ καθ᾽ ἕκαστον, a characteristic Thucydidean pairing of the grammatically nonparallel, can be taken either as adverbial or as appositive to βραχυτάτῳ κεφαλαίῳ.

τρία μὲν ὄντα. Accusative absolute. Sm. §2076.

37.1. The backbone of this sentence is Ἀναγκαῖον . . . μνησθέντας ἡμᾶς περὶ ἀμφοτέρων . . . καὶ ἰέναι ἐπὶ τὸν ἄλλον λόγον. Ἀναγκαῖον . . . μνησθέντας is interrupted by a long genitive absolute, which entails two clauses of indirect discourse following upon the word λόγον [argument]. The argument is specified by (a) περὶ τοῦ δέξασθαι (hence, "the argument about receiving them") and (b) the two clauses of indirect statement introduced by ὡς, which are in turn joined by καὶ . . . καὶ. This parallelism is marked by οὐ μόνον . . . ἀλλ᾽. A translation of the sentence follows.

> Since these Corcyreans have made an argument not only about receiving them but also that we are acting unjustly and that they themselves are unreasonably treated as enemies [i.e., that it is unreasonable that they should be brought to fighting], it is necessary for us, having first commented on both things, to move to the rest of the argument, so that . . .

μνησθέντας περί. "make mention concerning." LSJ s.v. μιμνήσκω B.II.

ἀξίωσιν and χρείαν are parallel and contrasting words meaning, roughly, "request." An ἀξίωσις is a worthy request from "us," and a χρεία is a desperate needful request from "them." An ἀξίωσις is a claim on the grounds of merit, whereas a χρεία is a claim on the grounds of necessity.

μὴ ἀλογίστως ἀπώσησθε. μή here applies not to the subjunctive verb (i.e., this is not a negative purpose clause) but only to the adverb, as a litotes. Hence, "in order that you may reject not unreasonably [i.e., with good reason]."

37.2. τὸ σῶφρον. Neuter adjective instead of abstract noun (the *schema Thucydideum*). Cf. **36.1.**

οὐδενός goes with ξυμμαχίαν as a possessive.

οὔτε παρακαλοῦντες αἰσχύνεσθαι (βουλόμενοι). "nor wishing to be ashamed when they ask for their support."

37.3. αὐτάρκη θέσιν κειμένη. "situated in an independent location." The present κεῖμαι serves as a substitute for the perfect middle (in passive sense) of τίθημι (Sm. §791); i.e., κειμένη is equivalent to the perfect middle τεθειμένη (rare or even unknown in Attic). θέσιν is a cognate accusative with τίθημι, except that τίθημι is represented by κειμένη. Sm. §1569. So θέσιν κειμένη means "situated in a situation." αὐτάρκη is the accusative singular feminine of the s-stem adjective αὐτάρκης, ⁻ες (self-sufficient, independent), which modifies θέσιν.

ὧν = τούτων οἷς. The antecedent, which would be genitive with δικαστάς (i.e., "judges of [cases]"), is omitted, and the relative pronoun whose case within its own clause ought to have been dative (i.e., "by means of which") is attracted to the case of its ghost antecedent. Sm. §2531a. Hence, "makes them judges of cases in which they . . ."

37.4. τὸ ἄσπονδον is a neuter adjective used instead of an abstract noun to mean "neutrality" and is the object of προβέβληνται.

The main verb προβέβληνται [put forward as a pretense for themselves] (LSJ s.v. B.III.2b) is followed by five purpose clauses.

οὐχ ἵνα μὴ ξυναδικῶσιν
ἀλλ' ὅπως . . . ἀδικῶσι
καὶ ὅπως μέν βιάζωνται
(δὲ) ἔχωσιν
(δὲ) ἀναισχυντῶσιν

οὗ δ' ἂν λάθωσι πλέον ἔχωσιν. "have more wherever they can get away with it." οὗ is the relative adverb meaning "where," not a genitive relative pronoun.

37.5. This sentence is a present contrary-to-fact condition: εἰ plus the imperfect indicative and the imperfect indicative plus ἄν. But there is no ἄν in the apodosis. "ἄν may be omitted in the apodosis of an unreal condition when the apodosis consists of an imperfect indicative denoting unfulfilled obligation, possibility, or propriety. Such are the impersonal expressions ἔδει, χρῆν, ἐξῆν, εἰκὸς ἦν, καλὸν ἦν etc. with the infinitive, the action of which is (usually) not realized" (Sm. §2313).

δίδουσι καὶ δεχομένοις. Dative plural participles modifying αὐτοῖς. The Corcyreans could have demonstrated their uprightness by granting just judgments to others and accepting just judgments themselves (but they did not).

38.1. διὰ παντός. Sc., χρόνου. Hence, "always, through all time."

38.2. τὰ εἰκότα θαυμάζεσθαι. "receive the customary marks of respect." LSJ s.v. θαυμάζω 2b. The middle of θαυμάζω means "be respected," and the neuter accusative τὰ εἰκότα is most easily explained as adverbial, meaning "with respect to the proper customary things."

38.4. εἰ . . . ἐσμέν . . . ἄν . . . ἀπαρέσκοιμεν. Mixed condition. The "if" clause is a real protasis ("if, as a matter of fact, . . ."), the first apodosis is a potential optative ("we would then . . ."), and the second apodosis returns with a present indicative to a real statement ("we now, as a matter of fact, are fighting . . ."). All of this is subordinate to δῆλον ὅτι.

μὴ . . . ἀδικούμενοι. "without being unjustly treated." The negative of the circumstantial participle is μή because it is tantamount to an "if" clause, which would take negative μή. Sm. §2728.

38.5. This sentence is a present contrary-to-fact condition, where the apodosis without ἄν consists of an imperfect indicative denoting an unfulfilled propriety. Cf. 37.5; Sm. §2313. The two apodoses without ἄν are καλὸν ἦν τοῖσδε and αἰσχρὸν ἦν ἡμῖν, and this contrast is marked by μέν . . . δέ. Each of the two neuter adjectives in the impersonal construction is defined by an infinitive, εἶξαι and βιάσασθαι. Strictly speaking, the infinitives are the subjects of ἦν, and the neuter adjectives are predicate adjectives.

κακουμένην. "being in distress, when it was in distress."

οὐ προσεποιοῦντο. "they did not try to lay claim to it." The meaning "try" comes from the verb's imperfect tense, sc., the "conative imperfect" (Sm. §1895). Alternatively, it may be regarded as an imperfect of resistance or refusal (Sm. §1896)—hence, "they refused to lay claim to it." The Corinthians are making a dog-in-the-manger argument here.

ἑλόντες βίᾳ ἔχουσιν. Where English prefers two coordinate verbs ("they took it by force and held it"), Greek usually prefers to put one of the verbs into a participle—hence, "having taken it by force, they held it."

39.1. The key to this sentence is δίκη, which here means "arbitration" and is the antecedent of the relative pronoun ἥν, the hook on which the rest of the sentence hangs. It is the object of προσκαλούμενον, which itself is one of the subjects of the infinitive δοκεῖν. The dependent clause introduced by ἥν has only one verb, δεῖ, and it is completed by the infinitive δοκεῖν, which itself has a complementary infinitive, λέγειν τι. οὐ negates δεῖ, but ἀλλά reverses the negation; i.e., "it is not proper for A and B, but it is proper for C." The infinitive δοκεῖν has three accusative subjects.

τὸν προύχοντα
καὶ ἐκ τοῦ ἀσφαλοῦς προκαλούμενον (δίκην)
ἀλλὰ τὸν . . . καθιστάντα

It is virtually impossible to translate this sentence into English literally with a relative clause in it, because of the peculiarly embedded position of ἥν, so one must make two sentences out of it, repeating the word *arbitration*.

> And indeed, they say that they were willing earlier to have the matter decided by arbitration. But it is not proper for the party in the advantageous position and proposing arbitration from a position of security to think he is saying something [meaningful], but, rather, it is proper for the party who puts his deeds and likewise his words on an equal basis [proposing arbitration] before entering into hostilities [to think he is saying something meaningful].

καθιστάναι ἐς ἴσον. "to bring into an equal state." LSJ s.v. καθίστημι A.II.3. The present active of καθίστημι must be transitive, and its objects are ἔργα and λόγους. Thus, the Corcyreans are to put their deeds and words on an equal state with those of their adversaries. But both Warner and Crawley take καθιστάντα to be intransitive as if it were the aorist participle καταστάντα, meaning "be in an equal position with respect to words and deeds." LSJ s.v. B5.

39.2. ἡγήσαντο ἡμᾶς οὐ περιόψεσθαι. "They realized that we were not going to overlook [the fact that they were besieging the place]."

οὐ ξυμμαχεῖν. The negative οὐ is used because it really belongs to ἀξιῶντες rather than to the infinitive, and it is placed after ἀξιῶντες for the sake of the contrast. Classen and Steup, ad loc.; Sm. §2738b.

39.3. The backbone of this sentence is χρῆν plus two infinitives, προ-ιέναι and ἔχειν. The accusative subject of the two infinitives is the Cor-cyreans, represented (a) by the accusative relative pronoun οὕς and (b) by the accusative participle κοινώσαντας. The first infinitive, προσιέναι, is modified by a series of temporal expressions, and the second infinitive, ἔχειν, is modified by the parallel temporal adverb πάλαι.

ἀπογενόμενοι. "keeping away from, have no part in" (plus the genitive). LSJ s.v. I.

τὰ ἀποβαίνοντα. "the consequences"—here, "consequences of policy, fortunes."

A translation of the sentence follows.

> They should have approached you then when they were most secure, not when we, on the one hand, are injured, and they, on the other hand, are at risk or when you are about to give a share of help, having at that time not had a share of their power, and when you are going to have an equal share of the blame from us, having hitherto kept yourselves aloof from their misdeeds; and only if they had long ago shared their power with you, should they have common fortunes [with you].

40.2. εἰ γὰρ εἴρηται. "granted the fact that it is specified." This "if" clause is not really conditional but concessive. Sm. §2369 ff. Usually, such clauses are introduced by εἰ καί.

ὅστις μή. When the antecedent of a relative clause is indefinite, the negative is μή. Sm. §2506.

40.3. μὴ ἄνευ ὑμῶν = μεθ' ὑμῶν. This is a meiosis (Sm. §3032). Hence, "If you attack with them, it will be necessary [for us] to defend ourselves against them and against you as well." In the middle, ἀμύνω means "ward off from oneself." LSJ s.v. B.1b.

40.4. δι' ἀνοκωχῆς γίγνεσθαι. "to be in a cease-fire with" (plus the dative). The preposition διά with genitive and stative verbs (e.g., εἶναι, ἔχειν, γίγνεσθαι) expresses a condition or state. LSJ s.v. A.IV.1a.

τὸν νόμον μὴ καθιστάναι. "not to establish the precedent." The precedent is defined by the result expression ὥστε plus the infinitive. Sm. §§2258, 2267.

40.5. εἰ χρή. Indirect question after δίχα ἐψηφισμένων.

40.6. φανεῖται καὶ ἃ τῶν ὑμετέρων οὐκ ἐλάσσω ἡμῖν πρόσεισι. "There will be some of your allies who will come over no less to us." The neuter plural relative ἃ with φανεῖται acts like a future of the expression ἔστιν ἃ (Sm. §2513) and is followed by the partitive genitive τῶν ὑμετέρων.

41.1. ἔχομεν has two sets of objects connected by μὲν . . . δέ: (a) δικαιώματα and (b) παραίνεσιν καὶ ἀξίωσιν. Then ἀξίωσιν χάριτος means "a claim on your gratitude" and is further modified by the relative clause introduced by ἥν—ἥν . . . ἀντιδοθῆναι ἡμῖν . . . φαμὲν χρῆναι "[which we say ought to be repaid to us]."

ἐπιχρῆσθαι. "have dealings with one." This rare word means "to have a mutual give and take, have dealings that expect a return." At Hdt. 3.99, the word suggests intimate friendship.

41.2. ὑπὲρ τὰ Μηδικά. "before the Persian War." LSJ s.v. ὑπέρ B.IV.

οἷς for ἐν οἷς. The preposition is not repeated. Sm. §1671.

41.3. τὰ οἰκεῖα χεῖρον τίθενται. "they value their own interests less." LSJ s.v. τίθημι B.II.

42.1. This sentence has two subjects: "you all" and the young person. The singular verb agrees with the second subject but applies to both. We would logically expect ἀξιοῦτε and μὴ νομίσητε. Sm. §§966, 968–69.

ἀξιούτω τοῖς ὁμοίοις ἡμᾶς ἀμύνεσθαι. "let him consider it right for us to be supported in a similar fashion [as we supported you in the affair of Aegina]."

42.2. The backbone of this sentence is a series of neuter adjectives.

τὸ ξύμφερον . . . ἕπεται
καὶ τὸ μέλλον . . . κεῖται
καὶ οὐκ ἄξιον . . . κτήσασθαι
σῶφρον (δὲ) ὑφελεῖν
  μηδ᾽ ἐφέλκεσθαι

ἕπεται is absolute (without any object) and means "is found in something," and the "something" is expressed by the ἐν ᾧ clause, meaning "where." LSJ s.v. *ἕπω II.4. Hence, "Expediency is most found wherever someone least makes a mistake."

τὸ μέλλον τοῦ πολέμου. "the future possibility of the war."

αὐτῷ. Sc., τὸ μέλλον τοῦ πολέμου.

ὑφελεῖν. ὑφαιρέω with a genitive means "take away part of something." LSJ s.v. II.2.

42.4. τοὺς ὁμοίους. I.e., powers as strong as yourselves, powers capable of retaliation.

τῷ αὐτίκα φανερῷ. "by something apparent at the moment," i.e., an immediate advantage that turns out to be a long-range disadvantage.

διὰ κινδύνων τὸ πλέον ἔχειν. διά with the genitive noun expressing manner, with the force of an adverb—hence, "riskily." Sm. §1685.1d; LSJ s.v. A.III.1c τὸ πλέον ἔχειν is contrasted with the earlier τὸ ἀδικεῖν. Hence, it is better not to harm other powers than to gain an advantage. τὸ πλέον ἔχειν or πλεονεξία (the active zeal to gain more and more power) is a thematic characteristic of the Athenians in Thucydides.

43.1. ἡμεῖς δὲ περιπεπτωκότες οἷς ἐν τῇ Λακεδαίμονι αὐτοὶ προείπομεν. The relative οἷς stands for τούτοις ἅ. περιπίπτω takes a dative of the circumstances met (LSJ s.v. II.3), and the relative, which logically should be accusative as the direct object of προείπομεν, is here attracted to the case of its ghost antecedent. Sm. §§2522, 2529, 2531. ἐν τῇ Λακεδαίμονι refers to the meeting at Sparta in which the Corinthians voted in favor of the Athenians in the matter of the Samian revolt (Thuc. I.41.2). The main verb of the sentence is ἀξιοῦμεν. Hence, "having fallen into the circumstances, . . . we think we deserve . . ."

44.1. ἐπιμαχίαν τῇ ἀλλήλων βοηθεῖν. An ἐπιμαχία is a merely defensive alliance, not a full-scale alliance; the latter would have included an obligation for the Athenians to join the Corcyreans in a directly offensive policy. ἐπιμαχία is defined by an infinitive alone. Sm. §1987. τῇ ἀλλήλων is for τῇ ἀλλήλων γῇ (cf. I.15.2, ἀπὸ τῆς ἑαυτῶν), dative after βοηθεῖν. A συμμαχία is an alliance that is both offensive and defensive, in which the parties swear to have the same friends and enemies; the Delian League is an example.

44.2. ξυγκρούειν. "cause [acc.] to wear out by collision with [dat.]." Hence, "they wanted to cause them to wear out by collision with each other."

ἤν τι δέῃ. "if ever it becomes necessary." This is an eventual condition. Sm. §2337. The sequence is primary despite the past leading verbs ἐδόκει and ἐβούλοντο.

καθιστῶνται. In II.75.1, Thucydides uses the transitive expression καθίστη ἐς πόλεμον τὸν στρατόν [sent his army into battle]; in I.23.6, he uses the intransitive aorist κατέστησαν ἐς πόλεμον [they went to war]. Here, the subjunctive middle intransitive καθιστῶνται means "in order that they may go to war [against those who are weaker]."

45.3. μὴ ναυμαχεῖν . . . κωλύειν. Infinitives after a verb of will or desire. Sm. §§1991, 1997.

46.1. αὐτοῖς. Dative of agent with pluperfect middle with passive meaning. Sm. §1488.

46.5. ὁρμίζονται. "came to anchor." LSJ s.v. II.

47.1. ἐστρατοπεδεύσαντο. In land contexts, στρατοπεδεύω means "to encamp," but in sea contexts, it means "to take a position" or, in the middle, "be stationed." LSJ s.v.

Σύβοτα. The name is neuter plural.

48.1. μετεώρους. This word usually means "in midair, aloft," but when applied to ships, it means "on the open sea." LSJ s.v. II.2.

48.3. τὸ δ' ἄλλο αὐτοὶ ἐπεῖχον τρία τέλη ποιήσαντες. "[The Corcyreans] themselves were extended along the other wing, having formed three squadrons." ἐπεῖχον means more than "hold," because it implies that the Corcyreans were extended. Cf. Thuc. III.107.4 for a parallel. The verb for the Athenians would have been ἦσαν if it were there. τρία τέλη ποιήσαντες means "having formed three squadrons." The Corcyreans formed the left, right, and middle of the battle line, with the Athenians in reserve beyond the Corcyrean right wing.

48.4. ἄριστα. Neuter plural accusative adjective used as an adverb. Sm. §1609.

49.1. ἀπειρότερον ἔτι. Adverb meaning "still in the inexperienced fashion" (in contrast to the modern fashion). The comparative adverb is used because two adverbial expressions are being compared by implication, sc., "in the modern way" and "in the old-fashioned, inexperienced way." Sm. §1080.

49.2. ἦν τε ἡ ναυμαχία καρτέρα, τῇ μὲν τέχνῃ οὐχ ὁμοίως (οὖσα). "The sea battle was fierce, [being] not so much [fierce] in technique, but being . . ."

49.3. διέκπλοι. The διέκπλους was a special naval tactic much employed later by the Athenians, which consisted in sailing through the enemy's line so as to ram their ships on the flank or in the rear (LSJ s.v.). Thucydides does not make the details of this maneuver very clear, but Polybius (1.51.9) describes it: διεκπλεῖν μὲν οὖν διὰ τῶν πολεμίων νεῶν καὶ κατόπιν ἐπιφαίνεσθαι τοῖς ἤδη πρὸς ἑτέρους διαμαχομένοις, ὅπερ ἐν τῷ ναυμαχεῖν ἐστι πρακτικώτατον κτλ. [to sail through the enemy's line and to appear from behind, while they were already fighting others [in front], which is a most effective naval maneuver . . .]. See R. B. Strassler, ed., *The Landmark Thucydides: A Comprehensive Guide to the Peloponnesian War* (New York: Free Press, 1996), appendix G ("Trireme Warfare in Thucydides").

49.4. εἴ πῃ πιέζοιντο. Past general condition. Sm. §2340. Hence, "if anywhere they were being pressed."

49.5. τρεψάμενοι. The middle of τρέπω is usually intransitive but is here transitive, meaning "having routed." LSJ s.v. III. Cf. Xen. *An.* 5.4.16.

49.7. ἔργου πᾶς εἴχετο. "everyone was taking a hand in the work [gen.]." LSJ s.v. ἔχω C.I.1.

διεκέκριτο οὐδὲν ἔτι. "there was no longer any distinction, any separation."

50.1. ἀναδούμενοι. In the middle, ἀναδέω means "take in tow." LSJ s.v. III.

καταδύσειαν is optative because it is in a general relative clause in secondary sequence. Sm. §2568. καταδύω is usually intransitive ("go down, set, sink"), but the aorist can be causative ("cause to sink, disable"). LSJ s.v. II.1.

50.2. ἐπὶ πολὺ τῆς θαλάσσης ἐπεχουσῶν. "extending over much sea." LSJ s.v. ἐπέχω V.

50.5. πρύμναν ἐκρούοντο. "backed water," i.e., reversed direction not by turning around but simply by rowing backward, stern first. LSJ s.v. κρούω 9.

51.2. πρίν τινες ἰδόντες εἶπον ὅτι . . . "until some people, upon seeing them, said that . . ." Sm. §2434.

51.4. προσκομισθεῖσαι. Feminine plural aorist passive participle of προσκομίζω. Hence, "making their way [through the wrecks]."

51.5. ὡρμίσαντο. "they anchored."

52.1. ἀναγαγόμενοι. In the middle, ἀνάγω, "lead up," means "put to sea." LSJ s.v. B.1.

52.2. ἄραντες. When applied to armies or fleets, αἴρω, "lift," means "get them under way, set sail." LSJ s.v. ἀείρω I.5.

αἰχμαλώτων τε περὶ φυλακῆς. There are two phrases in apposition to ἄπορα that define what those ἄπορα are: the prepositional phrase αἰχμαλώτων περὶ φυλακῆς and the parallel participial phrase ἐπισκευὴν οὐκ οὖσαν. The parallelism is marked by τε . . . καί.

ἐπισκευήν. "repair facilities."

52.3. τοῦ δὲ οἰκάδε πλοῦ. This genitive is proleptic, going logically with the indirect adverb ὅπῃ in the next clause ("in what direction of sailing home"), which introduces the indirect question. The genitive is used with adverbs (e.g., ὅπου γῆς). Sm. §1439. In the middle, κομίζω, "get, give heed to," can mean "travel, journey, get somewhere." LSJ s.v. II.4. In the passive, it means "get back or return." LSJ s.v. III. Hence, "They were more concerned with the question in what direction of sailing home they will get back."

ἑῶσι. Third plural subjunctive of an alpha-contract verb in a fearing clause; identical in form to the indicative. For the negative μὴ . . . οὐ in a negative clause of fearing (i.e., "[fearing] that not"), see Sm. §2221.

54.1. τὰ κατὰ σφᾶς ἐξενεχθέντα. The bodies and the wrecks had been carried back to the Corinthians by the current and the wind. The expression is related to the verb καταφέρω, which means "drive back to land." LSJ s.v. II.2. Cf. Thuc. IV.3.1. Cf. also I.54.2, τὰ κατὰ σφᾶς αὐτοὺς ναυάγια [The shipwrecks [that had washed] back to shore where they were].

56.2. ὅπως τιμωρήσονται αὐτούς. ὅπως with the future after a verb of effort (πρασσόντων). Sm. §§2209–11. αὐτούς refers to the Athenians.

ἐπιδημιούργους. "magistrates." This term was used specifically for the magistrates that Doric cities sent out to their colonies. Potidaea was a Corinthian colony, with annual magistrates sent out by Corinth, but it was also a member of the Delian League and a formal ally of Athens.

57.2. ἐπεπολέμωτο. "had been made an enemy, had been treated as an enemy." LSJ s.v. πολεμόω II. Gomme (ad loc.) says it means "was at war." But cf. Thuc. I.37.1, where πολεμοῦντο cannot mean "be at war" formally; there, it can only mean "treated as an enemy."

ἔπρασσεν . . . ὅπως γένηται. "Verbs of *effort* sometimes have the construction of final clauses, and take, though less often, ὅπως with the present or second [i.e., thematic] aorist subjunctive or optative. The subjunctive may be used after secondary tenses" (Sm. §2214).

αὐτοῖς. I.e., the Athenians.

57.5. εἰ . . . ἔχοι . . . ἂν . . . ποιεῖσθαι. Potential condition in indirect discourse after νομίζων. The secondary sequence is determined by the leading verb, the imperfect προσέφερε λόγους. The original direct form would be εἰ . . . ἔχοι, ποιοῖτο ἄν. Smyth does not adequately treat conditions in indirect discourse. In general, the apodosis becomes the corresponding infinitive (i.e., the infinitive of the same voice and aspect as the direct verb), and original independent verbs with ἄν (i.e., potential optatives, imperfects, and aorists) retain the ἄν when transformed to the infinitive. The protasis retains its original form, but general protases introduced by ἐάν may change from subjunctive to optative after secondary leading verbs (the optative option), losing their ἄν.

57.6. αὐτοῦ. I.e., Perdiccas.

†δέκα†. The daggers mean that the editor has despaired of fixing the text here. It is a *locus desperatus*. The issue is that this would mean eleven commanders on the same expedition, which the editor deems impossible. In I.116.1, Thucydides says that Pericles had nine colleagues in command in a sea battle off Tragia, which is reasonable because there were ten generals on the Board of Generals. But where would we get eleven? The favorite emendation is τεσσάρων (Krüger), on the paleographical grounds that the MS had δ, meaning "four," which was then interpreted wrongly as δ(έκα), "ten." The objection to that is that Δ is the older form for "ten" and may have been used by Thucydides himself. But see I.61.2, where Kallias sails to Macedonia with four colleagues in command.

ὅπως μὴ ἀποστήσονται. ὅπως μὴ with the future after a verb of effort. Sm. §§2209–11.

58.1. εἴ πως πείσειαν. "In case" clause with optative in secondary sequence. Sm. §2354. This clause sets forth the motive for the embassy.

[ἔπρασσον] ὅπως ἑτοιμάσαιντο. The editor has bracketed ἔπρασσον, indicating that he thinks it does not belong in the text. The main verb of the sentence is ἀφίστανται, and there is no room for another finite verb in this elegantly balanced sentence. The ὅπως ἑτοιμάσαιντο follows neatly after ἐλθόντες as a simple purpose clause in the optative in secondary sequence, and the ἔπρασσον is not needed.

The backbone of this sentence follows.

τότε ἀφίστανται
   πέμψαντες
     εἴ πως πείσειαν

ἐλθόντες
    ὅπως ἑτοιμάσαιντο
        ἦν δέῃ
ἐπειδὴ
    οὐδὲν [τε] ηὕροντο
    ἀλλ᾽
        ἔπλεον
        καὶ ὑπέσχετο
            ἐσβαλεῖν
                ἦν ἴωσιν

It is in primary sequence, but the aorist participles intervene and shift the clause εἴ πως πείσειαν and the clause ὅπως ἑτοιμάσαιντο to secondary sequence, because the aorist participles indicate a time before the main verb ("having sent, having gone"). Sm. §2176. The grammars do not make this principle clear.

ἐκ πολλοῦ πράσσοντες. "negotiating for a long time."

τὰ τέλη. "the authorities."

59.2. μετὰ Φιλίππου κτλ. "in cooperation with Philip."

61.1. τῶν πόλεων. Objective genitive—hence, "news about the cities." Sm. §1332. The news is explained by the following ὅτι clause.

61.3. ξύμβασιν ποιησάμενοι. "having made an agreement." The point is that they came to a convenient accommodation with Perdiccas and made the best deal they could, because the matter of Potidaea was more pressing.

61.4. χωρὶς δὲ τῶν ξυμμάχων πολλοῖς. Here, χωρὶς is not an improper preposition taking the genitive but a simple adverb, and τῶν ξυμμάχων is a partitive genitive with πολλοῖς, which is parallel to τρισχιλίοις. Hence, "with many of the allies besides." τρισχιλίοις and πολλοῖς are what Smyth calls, with picturesque precision, "datives of military accompaniment" (Sm. §1526).

61.5. κατ᾽ ὀλίγον δὲ προϊόντες. "advancing by short marches."

62.3. ἡ γνώμη τοῦ Ἀριστέως . . . ἔχοντι. *Constructio ad sensum.* ἔχοντι is dative even though it modifies τοῦ Ἀριστέως, because the expression ἡ γνώμη τοῦ Ἀριστέως is equivalent to ἔδοξε τῷ Ἀριστεῖ.

διακοσίαν ἵππον. When ἵππος is used as a collective noun meaning "cavalry," it is feminine. LSJ s.v. II.

62.4. ὅπως εἴργωσι τοὺς ἐκεῖθεν ἐπιβοηθεῖν. τοὺς ἐκεῖθεν, meaning "the people from there [sc., Olynthus]" (Sm. §1153e), is the subject of the infinitive ἐπιβοηθεῖν, meaning "bring aid." ἐπιβοηθεῖν is used absolutely, i.e., with no expressed object. Cf. Thuc. III.69.2. The whole infinitive phrase is the object of εἴργωσι. Hence, "in order to prevent the people from there from bringing aid." Sm. §2744.2.

62.6. λογάδες. "picked troops."

63.1. διακινδυνεύσῃ. Deliberative subjunctive in indirect discourse after ἠπόρησε. Hence, "He was at a loss [concerning] which of the two risks he should take."

ὡς ἐς ἐλάχιστον χωρίον. "over the shortest distance possible." Here, ὡς goes with the superlative. Sm. §1086.

παρὰ τὴν χηλήν. "along the breakwater." LSJ s.v. II. The scholiast here says: χηλὴ καλεῖται οἱ ἔμπροσθεν τοῦ πρὸς θάλασσαν τείχους προβε-βλημένοι λίθοι διὰ τὴν τῶν κυμάτων βίαν, μὴ τὸ τεῖχος βλάπτοιτο [The stones built out in front of the sea wall, so the wall is not damaged by the force of the waves, is called the *chele*].

βαλλόμενος. "under fire, being shot at."

64.1. τὸ ἐκ τοῦ ἰσθμοῦ [τεῖχος] . . . ἀποτειχίσαντες. ἀποτειχίζω means simply "fortify," "blockade," or, possibly, "build a counter wall." ἐκ τοῦ ἰσθμοῦ means "on the north side," i.e., toward the neck of the isthmus. It is contrasted with the following ἐς τὴν Παλλήνην, meaning "toward Pallene," i.e., toward the south. Pallene is the widened part of the penin-sula, contrasted with the narrow neck in the north. Heerwerden bracketed τεῖχος because it seemed superfluous, and the parallel phrase τὸ δ' ἐς τὴν Παλλήνην does not have it. Thus, the phrase means simply "the north side of the city," not "the north wall." It is not altogether clear what Thucydides means here. Gomme (p. 18) implies that the Athenians built a defensive wall around their camp on the north side of the city, i.e., not a circumvallation or a blockading wall. Crawley's translation reads, "The wall [of the city] on the side of the isthmus had now works at once raised against it." Warner's translation reads "The Athenians at once built and manned a counter wall to the north of the wall across the isthmus." But there is no wall "across the isthmus," and Warner seems to have misinterpreted ἐκ τοῦ ἰσθμοῦ. Classen and Steup (ad loc.) say, "The blockading of Potidaea by a besieging wall was accomplished in the following fashion: first the north and later also the south city wall were invested by a circumvallation; in the west and east where the city extended to the sea, blockade was only possible with ships." Whether Thucydides is talking about the city wall or the counter wall, whether the wall is no more than the defensive wall of the Athenian camp, and whether the wall extended across the isthmus are all unclear. But the following passage where the Athenians do not think they are strong enough to invest the south side of the city suggests a blockading wall, not merely the wall of the Athenian camp.

οἱ ἐν τῇ πόλει Ἀθηναῖοι. I.e., the Athenians back home in Athens.

65.1. ξυμβούλευε . . . τηρήσασι τοῖς ἄλλοις ἐκπλεῦσαι. "He counseled the others [except for five hundred defenders] to be on the lookout for a favorable wind and sail away."

τὰ ἐπὶ τούτοις. "what was necessary under these circumstances." LSJ s.v. ἐπί B.III.3; Sm. §1689.2c.

ὅπως . . . ἕξει. ὅπως with the future after a verb of effort (παρασκευά-ζειν). Sm. §2209–11.

65.2. ἔς τε Πελοπόννησον ἔπρασσεν ὅπῃ . . . γενήσεται. πράσσειν ἔς τινα means "to operate secretly." LSJ s.v. πράσσω I.6b. ὅπῃ plus the future is not strictly a clause of effort here, because it is not introduced by ὅπως. It behaves rather like an indirect question: "He intrigued how the help was going to come." But ὅπως and ὅπῃ are often linked in a fixed phrase, as in ὅπῃ ἔχει καὶ ὅπως (Pl. *Resp.* 612a), and it might be possible for an effort clause to be introduced by ὅπῃ.

66.1. ξυνερρώγει. Third singular pluperfect active intransitive of συρρή-γνυμι, "break, dash together." Hence, "had broken out."

ἀνοκωχή. "armistice, cease-fire."

ἰδίᾳ. "privately"—hence, "because the Corinthians had done these things on a private basis rather than as a matter of state policy." Officially, Aristaeus and his men were "volunteers" coming to the aid of the Chalcidians, rather than a formal expedition from Corinth in consequence of a formal alliance with the Chalcidians. Gomme, ad loc.

67.2. οὐκ εἶναι αὐτόνομοι κατὰ τὰς σπονδάς. The Thirty Years' Truce (445 B.C.), which brought to an end the so-called First Peloponnesian War, in which Pericles attempted to create a land empire and which culminated in the revolt of Euboea, specified among other things that the sovereignty and independence of Aegina be guaranteed. Alternatively, there may have been a separate treaty between Athens and Aegina, by which Aegina agreed to become a member of the Delian League.

67.3. ξύλλογον σφῶν αὐτῶν . . . τὸν εἰωθότα. The ordinary Spartan assembly to which all citizens over thirty years of age were admitted.

68.1. τὸ πιστόν. Neuter adjective instead of abstract noun (the *schema Thucydideum*). Hence, "confidence."

πολιτεία καὶ ὁμιλία. "constitution and way of life."

ἀπ᾽ αὐτοῦ. Sc., τοῦ πιστοῦ.

68.2. οὐ πρὶν πάσχειν. Sc., ἡμᾶς.

68.3. ὧν is here a complicated relative pronoun. It is genitive plural because it is partitive with the selecting phrases τοὺς μέν and τοῖς δέ. Hence, "some of whom you see already enslaved . . . against others of whom you see them [Athenians] plotting . . ." etc. Its antecedent is usually taken to be τὴν Ἑλλάδα by a *constructio ad sensum*—i.e., as meaning τοὺς Ἕλληνας. But there is an element of causality in the clause: it is equivalent to ἐπεὶ τῶν Ἑλλήνων . . . "since, you see that of the Greeks some . . ." Sm. §2555.

εἴ ποτε ἄρα πολεμήσονται. "In case" clause (which Smyth calls an "if haply" clause)—hence, "in case they will someday go to war." Sm. §2354. The combination εἰ ἄρα is used if the outcome is undesirable. Sm. §2796. Hence, "in case, heaven forbid, they will someday go to war."

68.4. γάϱ generally means that the preceding sentence requires explana-tion and that the sentence that follows will clear up the meaning. Hence, "What do we mean by saying that the Athenians are preparing in advance for war? Unless they are preparing for war, they would not . . ."

οὐ γὰϱ ἂν . . . εἶχον . . . ἐπολιόϱκουν. Potential imperfects, the indepen-dent part of a present contrary-to-fact condition. It is as if the protasis—i.e., the phrase "Unless they were preparing for war"—were suppressed. Sm. §§1784, 1786.

69.1. δουλωσάμενος. Here, this verb does not have passive meaning but means "make subject to oneself." Cf. Thuc. I.18.2, V.29.3, VII.68.2.

αὐτό. I.e., depriving the Greeks of liberty.

εἴπεϱ καὶ . . . φέϱεται. Real conditional clause with indicative, meaning "even if in fact." In the middle, φέϱω means "carry off as a prize, win." LSJ s.v. A.VI.3. The prize is the reputation for virtue.

69.2. ἐπὶ φανεϱοῖς. "on explicit terms, for clear purpose."

εἰ ἀδικούμεθα. Indirect question. Sm. §2671.

οἱ γὰϱ δϱῶντες . . . ἐπέϱχονται. "for efficient people, who have already made plans against those who are in a state of indecision, move without delay." ἤδη is to be taken with βεβουλευμένοι. καί connects βεβουλε-υμένοι and μέλλοντες, literally, "those who have made plans already and do not delay move."

69.3. κατ᾽ ὀλίγον. "little by little."

διὰ τὸ ἀναισθητόν. Neuter adjective for abstract noun (the *schema Thu-cydideum*). Hence, "on account of your lack of perception."

γνόντες δὲ εἰδότας πεϱιοϱᾶν. Both participles are conditional. Sm. §2067. Hence, "but if they recognize that if you do know, you overlook . . ." The point is that if the Athenians think that they are getting away with their aggression because the Spartans do not notice, the former will move care-fully, so as not to awaken the latter, but it will be even worse if the Athenians conclude that the Spartans do not even care and, thus, that no caution or hesitancy is necessary.

69.4. ἡσυχάζετε picks up the idea in the preceding εἰδότας πεϱιοϱᾶν. Hence, "you do nothing."

τινά. Object of ἀμυνόμενοι. In the middle, ἀμύνω means "defend oneself against" and takes an accusative of the person. LSJ s.v. B.I.b.

τῇ μελλήσει. "by being about to do something." The noun is related to the verb μέλλω, "to be about to, to delay."

69.5. καίτοι . . . ἐκράτει. "and yet you used to be called reliable, whose reputation [it turns out] exceeded your action." The relative clause marks a surprising conclusion because of ἄρα. "ἄρα is often used to indicate a new perception, or surprise genuine or affected; as when the truth is just realized after a previous erroneous opinion" (Sm. §2795).

τόν τε γὰρ Μῆδον κτλ. This sentence has three coordinate independent clauses connected by καί.

> ἴσμεν
> καὶ . . . περιορᾶτε
> καὶ . . . βούλεσθε

All the rest is dependent on one of these. The ἴσμεν clause takes an accusative and participle in indirect discourse after a verb of perception. Sm. §2106.

> ἴσμεν . . . τὸν Μῆδον . . . ἐλθόντα πρότερον
> ἢ τὰ παρ' ὑμῶν . . . προαπαντῆσαι.

πρότερον here acts like πρίν with the infinitive. Sm. §§2383c, 2458. τὰ παρ' ὑμῶν means "your defense forces" and is the subject of the infinitive προαπαντῆσαι.

ἀντὶ τοῦ ἐπελθεῖν αὐτοί. "instead of attacking yourselves." αὐτοί is the subject of the articular infinitive and is nominative because it refers to the subject of the main verb. Sm. §1973a.

Βούλεσθε has two complementary infinitives, ἀμύνεσθαι and καταστῆναι, and the subject is modified by two circumstantial participles, ἀγωνιζόμενοι and ἐπιστάμενοι. The latter is followed by two participles in indirect discourse after a verb of knowing with accusative subject (Sm. §2106), σφαλέντα and περιγεγενημένους.

The backbone of this sentence follows.

> Βούλεσθε
> ἀμύνεσθαι ἐπιόντας
> καὶ ἐς τυχὰς καταστῆναι

ἀγωνιζόμενοι πρὸς δυνατωτέρους
καὶ ἐπιστάμενοι
τὸν βάρβαρον σφαλέντα
καὶ ἡμᾶς περιγεγενημένους
ἐπεὶ . . . ἔφθειραν.

ἀμύνεσθαι ἐπιόντας. "to defend yourselves against the attackers."

ἐς τύχας . . . καταστῆναι. The intransitive aorist καταστῆναι means "to be in a certain state or position" and often occurs with the preposition ἐς, as in ἐς φόβον, ἐς δέος, ἐς τοὺς κινδύνους—hence, "to be in fear, to be at risk." LSJ s.v. καθίστημι B.V. ἀγωνιζόμενοι explains the risk. Hence, here, "to stand the risk of fighting people more powerful by far."

αἱ ὑμέτεραι ἐλπίδες. ὑμέτεραι stands for an objective ἐς ὑμᾶς, and the phrase means "hope placed in you." Sm. §1197.

69.6. μηδεὶς . . . νομίσῃ. Prohibitive subjunctive. Sm. §1800.

αἰτία. "expostulation"—i.e., a friendly remonstrance rather than an accusation. LSJ s.v. I.4. Classen and Steup translate, "Our suggestions are no κατηγορία but an αἰτία: for we are treating you as erring friends [φίλοι ἁμαρτάνοντες], not as enemies who have done wrong [ἐχθροὶ ἀδικήσαντες]; therefore regard our intention not as hostile, but as friendly."

70.1. εἴπερ τινὲς καὶ ἄλλοι. "if any others [are worthy—i.e., have a right—we certainly are]"; i.e., "if anybody has a right, we do."

ἄλλως τε καί. "especially."

ἐκλογίσασθαι . . . ἔσται. The indirect question after ἐκλογίζεσθαι is introduced by the question words οἵους and ὅσον. Classen and Steup paraphrase the indirect question as οἷοί εἰσιν Ἀθηναῖοι, πρὸς οὓς ὑμῖν ὁ ἀγὼν ἔσται, καὶ ὅσον καὶ ὡς πᾶν ὑμῶν διαφέρουσιν. But it is somewhat collapsed because the question word οἵους is the object of the preposition πρός, as is the participle διαφέροντας. Hence, "You do not seem ever to have considered what kind of men these Athenians are with whom you will have a fight or how much and how completely they are different from you."

70.2. ὀξεῖς. This adjective (meaning "quick, sharp, eager") and the epexegetical infinitives ἐπινοῆσαι and ἐπιτελέσαι, which apply to the Athenians, make logical sense. But the infinitives that apply to the Spartans hang in midair. They cannot logically be dependent on ὀξεῖς, since that would mean the Spartans were quick to do nothing. Maybe the Corinthians are being sarcastic and are really saying, "You are quick to keep what you have, thus initiate nothing, and quick to fail to bring to completion in actuality what is necessary."

ἔργῳ . . . τἀναγκαῖα ἐξικέσθαι. "to bring necessary things into action, to accomplish what is necessary." ἐξικνέομαι is ordinarily intransitive but here has transitive force. LSJ s.v. II.2.

70.3. παρά. "beyond." LSJ s.v. C.III.3.

τὸ δὲ ὑμέτερον "It is your thing [characteristic, habit] to . . ." (plus the infinitives πρᾶξαι, πιστεῦσαι, and οἴεσθαι).

70.4. καὶ μὴν καί. "and in truth also." Sm. §2921.

οἴονται . . . ἄν τι κτᾶσθαι . . . τὰ ἕτοιμα ἄν βλάψαι. The infinitives represent potential optatives in indirect discourse after οἴονται. The direct form would be, e.g., κτῴμεθα ἄν τι. Sm. §1845.

70.6. ἀλλοτριωτάτοις, meaning "completely belonging to another (here, to the city), expendable," is contrasted with οἰκειοτάτῃ, meaning "completely one's own." The point is that the Athenians treat their bodies as if they belonged to the state and were expendable, whereas their ingenuity, intelligence, thought, and opinions belong to themselves but are used for the benefit of the city.

70.7. ἃ μὲν . . . μὴ ἐπεξέλθωσιν and ἃ δ᾽ ἄν . . . κτήσωνται are general relative clauses in primary sequence with ἄν plus the subjunctive ("whatever" clauses). Sm. §2567.

ἡγοῦνται governs two infinitives of indirect discourse, στέρεσθαι (with no accusative subject, since its subject is the same as that of the leading verb) and τυχεῖν.

ὀλίγα πρὸς τὰ μέλλοντα. "little in comparison to future things." LSJ s.v. πρὸς C.III.4.

τυχεῖν πράξαντες is the familiar use of τυγχάνω with the participle to mean "to happen to do something," here used in indirect discourse after ἡγοῦνται. Hence, "they think they happen to have achieved little . . ." The participle is nominative because it refers to the subject of the leading verb. But τυγχάνω with the participle can express a coincidence in time "just now." LSJ s.v. II.1. So we may translate, "they think they have achieved little just then in comparison with things to come."

ἀντελπίσαντες. "hoping instead"—i.e., as a substitute for the failed enterprise.

ἐπλήρωσαν τὴν χρείαν. ἐπλήρωσαν is an "empiric" aorist. "With adverbs signifying *often, always, sometimes, already, not yet, never*, etc., the aorist expressly denotes a fact of experience" (Sm. §1930). There is no such adverb here, but the eventual conditional protasis and the presence of the word πεῖρα are sufficient. χρεία here means "lack, loss." Hence, "they always make up the loss." Note that this "empiric" aorist does not cause the conditional clause to change to secondary sequence.

70.8. This sentence has two independent clauses, with the verbs μόχθουσι and ἀπολαύουσι. Dependent on the latter is the preposition διά, followed by two articular infinitives, κτᾶσθαι and ἡγεῖσθαι. After ἡγεῖσθαι is a predicative construction without εἶναι, consisting of two accusatives ("to think A is B").

> ἡγεῖσθαι
>> ἑορτὴν = μήτε ἄλλο
>>> ἢ τὰ δέοντα πρᾶξαι
>> ἡσυχίαν τε = οὐχ ἧσσον ξυμφορὰν
>>> ἢ ἀσχολίαν.

Hence, "because they consider a holiday nothing else than to do what is necessary, and [because they consider] leisurely peace and quiet no less a trouble than [is] laborious activity."

70.9. ξυνελών. "summarizing, speaking concisely, in a word." LSJ s.v. συναιρέω I.2b.

71.1. The backbone of this sentence follows.

> διαμέλλετε
> καὶ οἴεσθε
>> τὴν ἡσυχίαν ἀρκεῖν
>>> οὐ τούτοις

οἱ ἂν . . . πράσσωσι
καὶ οἱ [ἂν] δῆλοι ὦσι
ἀλλ᾽ . . . νέμετε . . . τὸ ἴσον
    ἐπὶ
    τῷ μὴ λυπεῖν
    καὶ μὴ βλάπτεσθαι

οὐ τούτοις τῶν ἀνθρώπων. Partitive genitive with pronoun. Sm. §1317. The negative applies only to τούτοις. Hence, "not to those who . . . , but you . . ."

ἀρκεῖν. From the meaning "be sufficient," this verb came to mean "last, endure." LSJ s.v. III.4.

οἳ ἂν τῇ μὲν πρασκευῇ δίκαια πράσσωσι. "whoever act justly in their preparation for war."

μὴ ἐπιτρέψοντες. This construction is absolute (i.e., without object) and means "not submitting, not giving in." The negative is μή because the participle is embedded in the conditional clause ἢν ἀδικῶνται.

The parallelism is between τῇ μὲν παρασκευῇ [preparations] and τῇ δὲ γνώμῃ [will/determination], i.e., between acting justly in whatever preparations for war there are and being firm in their resolve if they are harmed. These are the positive attitudes the Corinthians would like to see in the Spartans.

ἐπὶ τῷ μὴ λυπεῖν . . . τὸ ἴσον νέμετε. "You exercise fairness on the basis of not injuring . . . and not being injured." Crawley translates, "Your ideal of fair dealing is based on the principle that . . ." τὸ ἴσον is a neuter adjective used instead of an abstract noun (the *schema Thucydideum*). The verb νέμω basically means "distribute, dispense" and came to mean "manage, inhabit, possess, etc." Its meaning here, "exercise, practice," is unusual—and, indeed, is omitted from LSJ—but τὸ ἴσον νέμετε is parallel to the earlier δίκαια πράσσωσι and is similar to Thucydides' usage in I.120.1: τὰ ἴδια ἐξ ἴσου νέμοντας [administering private interests equitably].

αὐτοὶ ἀμυνόμενοι. The subject of the infinitive is nominative because it refers to the subject of the leading verb νέμετε. Sm. §1973.

71.2. μόλις δ᾽ ἂν πόλει ὁμοίᾳ παροικοῦντες ἐτυγχάνετε τούτου. Potential imperfect. Sm. §1784. Hence, "You would acquire this [i.e., to harm none and not to be harmed] with difficulty [even if] you lived next to a city like [yours; i.e., with the same nonaggressive policy]."

ὥσπερ τέχνης. "as of an art or craft, [so in politics]."

τὰ ἐπιγιγνόμενα κρατεῖν. "The emerging new facts [of a craft] prevail [over the old-fashioned]." τὰ ἐπιγιγνόμενα has to be the subject of κρατεῖν, because any object would have been genitive. Here, κρατεῖν is used absolutely.

πολλῆς καὶ τῆς ἐπιτεχνήσεως δεῖ. πολλῆς is in predicate position. Sm. §1169. Hence, "there is need for innovation to be abundant."

71.4. ὡρίσθω. Third singular perfect middle imperative of ὁρίζω, "put a boundary to." The omega results from the lengthening of the initial vowel of ὁρίζω to form the perfect stem, an analogue to reduplication in verbs beginning with a single consonant. (It must not be called an augment. Augments have a different origin and signal past tense.) Hence, "let your slowness be put an end to." (An archaic English construction frequent in Jane Austen is useful here for illustrating the Greek syntax. Jane said somewhere, e.g., "What shall he be done to?" In such a transformation, the object of an English preposition becomes the subject of the sentence.)

προῆσθε. Second plural aorist middle subjunctive of προίημι. The aorist stem of ἵημι is ἑ- (from *ye-), and the subjunctive morpheme is ⁻η/ω⁻, so *γέ⁻η⁻σθε becomes ⁻ἦσθε (it occurs only in compounds).

71.5. δι' ἐρημίαν. "from being left alone."

72.1. παριτητέα. Neuter plural verbal adjective in ⁻τέος expressing necessity. Sm. §§471, 473. The use of the neuter plural is peculiar to Thucydides. It is formed from the verb πάρειμι, a compound of εἶμι, "go." This construction usually acts like the impersonal passive periphrastic in Latin (e.g., *eundum est mihi*, "I must go") and ordinarily has a dative of agent. Sm. §1488. But here, the participle ἀπολογησομένους has drifted over into the accusative. Schwyzer-Debrunner, 410. (αὐτοῖς goes with ἔδοξεν.) The normal verbal of εἶμι is ἰτέον, but this is from the secondary formation *ἰτητέω (Schwyzer, 705). Cf. Ar. *Nub.* 131. Either the neuter plural or the neuter singular of the verbal may be used in the impersonal construction, with no difference of meaning. Goodwin-Gulick §§1596–99 (here more helpful than Sm.).

καὶ ἅμα τὴν σφετέραν πόλιν ἐβούλοντο σημῆναι ὅση εἴη δύναμιν. "Lilies-of-the-field" construction.

ὧν ᾔδεσαν and ὧν ἄπειροι ἦσαν follow ὑπόμνησιν. Hence, "to remind the elders of what they knew and to give indication to the young of what they have not experienced." The first relative takes its genitive case from the ghost antecedent. The filled-out expression would be ὑπόμνησιν ἐκείνων ἃ κτλ. The second relative is genitive (a) from the ghost antecedent and (b) because ἄπειρος takes a genitive. LSJ s.v.

νομίζοντες... ἂν... τράπεσθαι. Potential optative in indirect discourse. Sm. §1845.

72.2. εἴ τι μὴ ἀποκωλύοι. Real condition in indirect discourse in secondary sequence after past leading verb. The direct form would be βουλό-μεθα... εἴ τι μὴ ἀποκωλύει, "If there is no objection, we want to speak." This indirect form then means "They said that if there was no objection, they wanted to speak." Smyth's treatment of conditional clauses in indirect discourse leaves much to be desired, but see Sm. §2619.

73.1. ἡμῶν with καταβοήν. "against us."

παρήλθομεν... οὐ... ἀνεροῦντες. This future participle signifies purpose after a verb of motion (Sm. §2065) and is parallel with the negative purpose clause ὅπως μὴ... βουλεύσησθε.

73.2. ὧν ἀκοαὶ μᾶλλον λόγων μάρτυρες ἢ ὄψις τῶν ἀκουσομένων. The contrast is between the direct experience of the audience (a better argument) and the ancient tales (not so convincing). Here, too, is a grammatical play of singulars and plurals, which may seem confusing. ἀκοαί [hearsay] is plural because its modifying genitive, λόγων, is plural. Hence, "of which stories hearsay is the witness, rather than the direct observation of those who are going to listen [to us]." ὧν is a relative adjective modifying λόγων, which is the incorporated antecedent. Sm. §2536. ἀκούω is deponent in the future.

εἰ καὶ δι᾽ ὄχλου μᾶλλον ἔσται. δι᾽ ὄχλου εἶναι means "be or become troublesome." LSJ s.v. ὄχλος II. The entire phrase is a kind of real condition with future indicative, which Smyth classifies (on the basis of its translation) as a "concessive clause" (Sm. §2375). This is not the so-called emotional future condition (Sm. §2328) but simply a real condition meaning "Even if it is going to be troublesome...," "Granted that it will be troublesome...," or "Although it will be troublesome..." The combination εἰ καί makes it "concessive."

προβαλλομένοις. Sc., ἡμῖν. Hence, "Although it will be rather trouble-some [tiresome] for us referring constantly to things that . . ." LSJ s.v. προβάλλω B.III.2. Some editors argue for the translation "tiresome to you," but the middle seems to argue against it.

ὅτε ἐδρῶμεν. Definite past temporal clause with indicative denoting the same time as the principal verb (ἐκινδυνεύετο). Hence, "When we were actually doing this . . . , the risk was being taken . . ." Sm. §2395A.

ἐπ᾽ ὠφελίᾳ. "for a [certain] advantage." LSJ s.v. ἐπί B.III.2 (of an end or purpose). The rest of the sentence is dependent on the word ὠφελίᾳ, the antecedent of the relative pronoun ἧς, which is followed by two other dependent genitives linked by μέν and δέ, τοῦ μὲν ἔργου and τοῦ δὲ λόγου. τοῦ μὲν ἔργου is a defining genitive of the neuter noun μέρος, and τοῦ δὲ λόγου is the genitive complement of the verb στερισκώμεθα, a verb in -ίσκω derived from στερέω. Sm. §§526–28. Hence, "a part of the actual outcome of which [i.e., the good] you share in, but let us not be deprived of all of the credit." In Thucydides, the word ἔργον tends to refer to actualities, facts, realities, brass tacks, material advantage, action—as opposed to λόγος, which refers to words, promises, theories, pretenses, reputation, talk. LSJ s.v. λόγος VI.2d.

εἴ τι ὠφελεῖ. Real condition with present indicative. Hence, "if [in fact] reputation is an advantage."

73.3. μὴ εὖ βουλευομένοις. The negative μή is used because the parti-ciple is equivalent to a conditional clause. Sm. §2728.

73.4. ἔσχε μὴ . . . αὐτόν . . . πορθεῖν. "prevented him from sacking." LSJ s.v. ἔχω A.II.10. For a summary of constructions after verbs of hindering, see Sm. §2744.

ἀδυνάτων ἂν ὄντων. Although this looks like a simple genitive absolute, it is only an attributive genitive, modifying the implied τῶν Πελοποννησίων in the word τὴν Πελοπόννησον. ἄν indicates that the original form was a potential optative or contrary-to-fact condition. Sm. §1845. The context indicates a contrary-to-fact condition, i.e., ἀδύνατοι ἂν ἦσαν. Hence, "in which case [i.e., if he had sacked the cities of the Peloponnesus] they [the Peloponnesians] would have been unable to come to each others' aid against so many ships." The imperfect is used in a past contrary-to-fact condition (where we expect the aorist) if the action was continuous or habitual. Sm. §2304. "Being unable" is such a continuous state.

73.5. ὡς . . . οὐκέτι . . . οὔσης. Genitive absolute with ὡς, indicating that this was the opinion or ground of action of the barbarian. Sm. §2086.

74.1. αἰτιώτατος. "most responsible, most to be credited with, most instrumental in causing."

ὅπερ. Sc., τὸ ναυμαχῆσαι.

74.2. τῶν ἄλλων ἤδη μέχρι ἡμῶν δουλευόντων. "the others as far as Attica [literally, "up to us"] being already slaves [to the Persians]."

ἠξιώσαμεν [we resolved] is followed by four infinitives.

μηδ' . . . προλιπεῖν
μηδὲ . . . γενέσθαι
ἀλλ' . . . κινδυνεῦσαι
καὶ μὴ ὀργισθῆναι

μηδ' ὡς . . . προλιπεῖν. "not even under those circumstances [when nobody came to our aid and all were enslaved] to abandon the alliance." Notice the accentuation of ὡς, the demonstrative adverb. Sm. §2988.

οὐ προυτιμωρήσατε. "You did not come to our aid earlier."

74.3. ὥστε φαμὲν οὐχ ἧσσον αὐτοὶ ὠφελῆσαι ὑμᾶς ἢ τυχεῖν τούτου. "Consequently, we claim that we ourselves helped you no less than we gained this [help from you]"—i.e., "We gave as much help as we received." The appearance of ὥστε at the beginning of a sentence marks a strong conclusion. LSJ s.v. B.II.2.

ἀπό τε τῶν οἰκουμένων τῶν πόλεων καὶ ἐπὶ τῷ τὸ λοιπὸν νέμεσθαι. "[You came to our aid] from inhabited cities and for the purpose of inhabiting [them] in the future." For ἐπί plus the dative articular infinitive to express aim or purpose, see LSJ s.v. B.III.2; cf. Thuc. I.38.2. In the middle, νέμω means "inhabit." LSJ s.v. A.III.1.

οὐχ ἡμῶν τὸ πλέον. Ironic—i.e., "You did not fear more for us than for yourselves."

ἀπὸ τῆς οὐκ οὔσης ἔτι. Understand πόλεως.

τὸ μέρος. Neuter accusative used as an adverb, meaning "partly." Sm. §§1606, 1609. It is linked to the element of joint effort in ξυνεσώσαμεν and implies, "we did our part in saving both you and ourselves." Cf. Thuc. I.127.2.

ὡς διεφθαρμένοι. ὡς plus the participle to express the opinion of the subject. Sm. §2086. διεφθαρμένοι is the nominative plural masculine perfect middle participle of διαφθείρω. Hence, "in the belief that we were already in the state of having been completely ruined."

75.1. Ἆρ' marks a question. Sm. §2650. Ἆρα μή marks a question expecting the answer no. Hence, "We don't deserve to be envied, do we?" Sm. §2651. However, Denniston (*Gr. Part.*², 46–47) argues that Ἆρα μή does not expect the answer no but simply is used in rhetorical questions and that it merely implies "that the suggestion made is difficult of acceptance." He interprets the present passage as expecting the answer yes, with μή negating only the infinitive. Hence, "Do we not deserve not to be envied?" He also observes that this is the only example of Ἆρα in Thucydides.

γνώμης ξυνέσεως ἕνεκα. "because of the correct insight of our decisiveness."

ἀρχῆς . . . τοῖς Ἕλλησι . . . ἐπιφθόνως διακεῖσθαι. The verb διακεῖμαι, "to be in a certain state," is frequently used with an adverb that defines the state. Hence, "to be in a state of being envied." The adjective ἐπίφθονος means "liable or subject to envy." The phrase ἐπιφθόνως διακεῖσθαι takes a dative of the person who is envious and a genitive of the cause of the envy. Sm. §1405. Hence, "We do not deserve to be envied by the Greeks for our hegemony, do we?" or, following Denniston (*Gr. Part.*², p. 47), "Do we not deserve to be free of envy for our hegemony?"

ἀρχῆς γε. γε implies that while there may be other reasons for envy, the Athenians' hegemony, at least, should not be begrudged them. Sm. §2821.

75.3. προαγαγεῖν αὐτὴν ἐς τόδε. "to advance [our hegemony] to this degree."

μάλιστα ὑπὸ δέους, ἔπειτα καὶ τιμῆς, ὕστερον καὶ ὠφελίας. "mostly out of fear [of Persia], then out of honor [of being head of the hegemony], and finally out of self-interest [the material and political advantage gained from such a position]."

75.4. Καὶ οὐκ ἀσφαλὲς κτλ. The backbone of this sentence (without the embedded genitive absolutes) follows.

οὐκ ἀσφαλὲς . . . ἔδοκει
  (ἡμᾶς)
  ἀπηχθημένους
  ἀνέντας
  κινδυνεύειν

ἀνέντας is the accusative plural aorist active participle of ἀνίημι. The two participles in the sentence are not really parallel. The first, ἀπηχθημένους, is a circumstantial (causal) participle ("since we were . . .") and is logically parallel to the genitive absolutes. The second, ἀνέντας, is a supplementary participle linked with the infinitive κινδυνεύειν; i.e., ἀνέντας κινδυνεύειν means "to take the risk consisting of letting it go." Sm. §§2094–2105. The meaning is clearer if we transform the expression out of the infinitive construction into a finite construction. It is like ἀδικῶ ταῦτα ποιῶν, "I am guilty in doing this." Sm. §2101. So κινδυνεύω ἀνείς means "I run the risk of letting go." Thus, the whole construction means "It did not seem safe [for us] to run the risk of letting go." Finally, ἀνιέναι is used absolutely; i.e., it is a transitive verb without its expected object "hegemony," which can be easily supplied from the course of the discussion.

καὶ γὰρ ἂν κτλ. γάρ signals that this sentence will explain what was meant by κινδυνεύειν. ἐγίγνοντο is imperfect (where we expect aorist, for past potential) because it refers to repeated events. Sm. §2304.

75.5. πᾶσι ἀνεπίφθονον τὰ ξυμφέροντα τῶν μεγίστων πέρι κινδύνων εὖ τίθεσθαι. In the middle, εὖ τίθεσθαι means "to administer something well for oneself." LSJ s.v. τίθημι A.VII.1. τὰ ξυμφέροντα means "advantageous, expedient things" but here has a whiff of the predicative—hence, "to manage things well for ourselves so that they turn out to be advantageous." To do this is ἀνεπίφθονον to everybody, i.e., "not a cause for reproach." Hence, "Nobody can reproach us for managing to our best advantage affairs that concern the greatest risks."

76.1. γοῦν introduces an argument made with specific examples—hence, "You Lacedemonians, for instance, . . ." Sm. §2830; Denniston Gr. Part.², 451 f. This usage of γοῦν has picked up the nickname "part proof," because it confirms a preceding statement not with full argument but with a specific, telling example of its truth.

καὶ εἰ τότε . . . κινδυνεύειν. This is a mixed contrary-to-fact condition in indirect discourse after εὖ ἴσμεν μή. The protasis, εἰ ἀπήχθεσθε, is past contrary-to-fact with aorist, and the apodoses are present contrary-to-fact with imperfects represented by infinitives with ἄν.

The backbone of this sentence follows.

> εὖ ἴσμεν μὴ
>   ὑμᾶς ἢ ἄρχειν ἄν
> ἢ κινδυνεύειν ἄν
>   εἰ ἀπήχθεσθε

The negative μή is unusual, since the negative of the infinitive in indirect discourse is regularly οὐ. But μή is often used after leading verbs of strong asseveration or belief, such as εὖ ἴσμεν or μαρτυρέω, "bear witness." Sm. §2725.

ἀπήχθεσθε is the second plural aorist middle of ἀπαχθάνομαι, "be hated, incur hatred." Some editors and many MSS read the pluperfect ἀπήχθησθε, which would be parallel with the earlier perfect participle ἀπηχθημένους. αὐτούς [yourselves] emphasizes that the Lacedaemonians would themselves have acted just as the Athenians did.

A translation of the sentence follows.

> And if then you had remained in your position of leadership for the whole time and had become detested, as we are, we are certain that you would have become no less severe to your allies and would be compelled either to rule harshly or to find yourselves at risk.

76.2. The main verb of this sentence is πεποιήκαμεν, and everything is dependent on it. The Athenians are represented by the nominative participles and the "if" clauses, but after the "until" clause (μέχρι οὗ), the subject switches to the Spartans. There is an embedded genitive absolute and an embedded accusative absolute.

The backbone of this sentence follows.

> πεποιήκαμεν οὐδὲν θαυμαστὸν
>   εἰ ἐδεξάμεθα
>   καὶ μὴ ἀνεῖμεν
>   ἀλλ᾽ νομίζοντες
>   καὶ δοκοῦντες
> μέχρι οὗ
>   χρῆσθε τῷ λόγῳ
>   (ὃν προθεὶς) οὐδεὶς ἀπετράπετο.

καθεστῶτος. Genitive singular neuter perfect active participle of καθί-στημι in a genitive absolute consisting of the participle alone without a noun. Sm. §2072b. This is an impersonal construction followed by an infinitive phrase. Hence, "it being an established rule for the weaker to be hemmed in by the stronger." LSJ s.v. καθίστημι B.6.

τῷ δικαίῳ λόγῳ νῦν χρῆσθε. "now you appeal to the argument from justice."

παρατυχὸν ἰσχύι τι κτήσασθαι. Accusative absolute. Sm. §2076. Hence, "there being a chance to acquire something by force."

προθείς. Nominative singular masculine aorist active participle of προ-τίθημι, "advance as a principle, propose." LSJ s.v. II.4. Some editors prefer the meaning "put before, prefer to" (LSJ s.v. IV.3) and understand a genitive of comparison in τῆς ἰσχύος—hence, "no one preferring which [i.e., to force]."

οὐδείς πω . . . ἀπετράπετο. "Nobody who put forth the argument from justice was ever diverted from acquiring more" or, by the other interpreta-tion, "Nobody was ever diverted from acquiring more by preferring the argument from justice [to that of strength]."

76.3. οἵτινες χρησάμενοι . . . γένωνται. If we accept the reading of some MSS and Stuart Jones, γένωνται is an aorist subjunctive in a general relative clause without ἄν—hence, "those who [are of such a kind as to] employ." This construction, without ἄν, is common in Homer and occurs occasionally in Attic prose. Cf. Thuc. III.43.5, IV.17.2, IV.18.4. Sm. §2567b. But other editors read with other MSS the perfect γεγένηνται, making this a simple indicative relative clause (Sm. §§2553, 2562), mean-ing "those who, as a matter of fact, are in the present enduring state of actually employing."

76.4. ἄλλους γ᾽ ἂν οὖν οἰόμεθα τὰ ἡμέτερα λαβόντας δεῖξαι ἂν μάλι-στα εἴ τι μετριάζομεν. The first ἄν is anticipatory, preparing us for the upcoming ἄν with δεῖξαι, which represents a potential optative. Sm. §1765. λαβόντας is a conditional participle, meaning "if they took over." Sm. §2067. εἴ τι μετριάζομεν [whether we are at all moderate] is an indirect question after δεῖξαι and is equivalent to ὅσον μετριάζομεν, "how moderate we are." οὖν is inferential and "signifies that something follows from what precedes" (Sm. §2964).

ἐκ τοῦ ἐπιεικοῦς. Neuter adjective for abstract noun (the *schema Thucydideum*)—hence, "from moderation, fairness."

περιέστη. The intransitive root aorist of περιίστημι, "surround," used here metaphorically with the dative, i.e., "surrounded us, stood around us." LSJ s.v. B.I.3. Hence, "resulted."

77.1. ἐν ταῖς ξυμβολαίαις πρὸς τοὺς ξυμμάχους δίκαις. I.e., in lawsuits conducted according to treaties between allied states.

παρ' ἡμῖν αὐτοῖς ἐν τοῖς ὁμοιοῖς νόμοις ποιήσαντες τὰς κρίσεις. "establishing courts here [by us in Athens] according to the similar laws [as we ourselves are judged]."

The speaker seems to be giving two instances of Athenian ἐπιείκεια (fairness): (1) they themselves lose occasionally in the treaty courts (showing fairness) and (2) when trials are held at Athens, the allies are judged on the same basis as Athenians. The question is complicated both philologically and historically. One question is whether Thucydides, rather than indicating two instances of ἐπιείκεια, is saying that at one time, cases were tried in treaty courts, but now that they have been transferred to Athens, the allies still are treated fairly (one instance of ἐπιείκεια). Gomme's long note on the matter (p. 243) should be consulted.

> "Yet if we translate Thucydides' sentence in what seemed to be the most natural way, we must assume that between Athens and many, at least, of the subject states αἱ συμβολαί had been abolished, though we have no explicit evidence of this and the case of Mytilene—so soon after her drastic punishment—would be a surprising exception. The other alternative is to suppose, with many scholars, that Thucydides *is* giving two examples of Athenian ἐπιείκεια—her submission to (unjust) verdicts in many δίκαι ἀπὸ συμβολῶν where these take place in allied courts, and her establishment of impartial courts (for other cases) at home."

77.2. The backbone of this sentence includes an indirect question.

οὐδεὶς σκοπεῖ
    διότι
        οὐκ ὀνειδίζεται.

Hence, "no one considers why the charge is not made." διότι is usually a conjunction but here an indirect interrogative. LSJ s.v. I.2.

τοῦτο οὐκ ὀνειδίζεταί (τινι). τοῦτο refers to φιλοδικεῖν. The construction with ὀνειδίζω is an accusative of reproach and a dative of the accused against whom the reproach is leveled. Here in the passive transformation, the accusative charge τοῦτο becomes nominative and the datives remain, namely, the participles ἔχουσι and οὖσι.

πρὸς ἡμᾶς ἀπὸ τοῦ ἴσου ὁμιλεῖν. "have dealings with us on an equal basis." LSJ s.v. ὁμιλέω A.III.1.

77.3. παρὰ τὸ μὴ οἴεσθαι χρῆναι. There is much confusion about the meaning of this phrase. Somehow it must be made to mean "contrary to what they think is right," but the μή is troublesome, and the παρά is ambiguous. The point is that the allies are so used to being treated on an equal basis that when they are overruled in the courts or by imperial power, instead of being thankful they did not lose more, they resent their subject status. παρά can mean "contrary to" (LSJ s.v. C.III.4) or "in accordance with" (LSJ s.v. C.I.7), and μή could go with οἴεσθαι or with χρῆναι. I think it best to take παρά as "in accordance with" and μή as the simple negative with the articular infinitive οἴεσθαι. Hence, "in accordance with the fact that they do not think it ought to be."

ἢ γνώμῃ ἢ δυνάμει τῇ διὰ τὴν ἀρχήν. "either by some legal decision made by us or by reason of the power we wield by virtue of our hegemony."

οὐ τοῦ πλέονος μὴ στερισκόμενοι χάριν ἔχουσιν. "They are not thankful that they are not deprived of more." οὐ negates χάριν ἔχουσιν, and μὴ negates στερισκόμενοι, which is a supplementary participle giving the reason or cause for thanks. It is parallel to supplementary participles with verbs of rejoicing and grieving, which give the ground for the emotion. Sm. §2100. The negative is μὴ because the reason for the action is regarded as the condition under which it takes place. Sm. §2731.

τοῦ ἐνδεοῦς χαλεπότερον φέρουσιν. χαλεπῶς φέρειν means "take ill, take amiss, get indignant at." LSJ s.v. φέρω A.III.2. χαλεπότερον is the comparative of the adverb χαλεπῶς. Sm. §345. The genitive τοῦ ἐνδεοῦς goes with the χαλεπότερον φέρουσιν—hence, "they are more indignant about their loss." It is a genitive of cause with expressions of emotion. Sm. §1405. For the genitive with the adverb, cf. Thuc. II.62.3. Thus, instead of being thankful for the greater part that they have, they are more indignant about the smaller part that has been taken away from them, the "part lacking," and they are more concerned about that "than if we habitually were . . ."

εἰ . . . ἐπλεονεκτοῦμεν. We would expect a past contrary-to-fact protasis here with the aorist ("than if we had . . ."). But it is imperfect here because it is contrary not only to a present reality but also to a continuous reality in the past. Cf. Thuc. I.11.2. Hence, "if we had been in the custom of . . ." Sm. §2304.

ἐκείνως. "under those conditions, in that case"—sc., if the Athenians ignored the law and openly aggrandized.

77.4. πλεονεκτεῖσθαι. In the active, πλεονέκτέω means "gain some advantage, get a larger share, grasp for more." In the middle, it means "be taken advantage of." LSJ (s.v. II.2) explains this usage as impersonal ("to be an act of πλεονεξία"), but it is parallel to καταναγκάζεσθαι, which is personal.

77.5. γοῦν indicates that what follows explains what was meant by the last general statement by giving a particular instance of its truth. Sm. §2830.

ἠνείχοντο. Third plural imperfect middle of ἀνέχω, "hold up, endure." In the middle, it means "bear up with patience." LSJ s.v. C.II.1. It has a double augment, both the preverb ἀνα⁻ and the root .ἐχ⁻ being augmented. Sm. §451.

εἰκότως is added as an afterthought with the meaning "fairly understandably after all" and leads to the next explanatory generalization.

77.6. This sentence begins as a straightforward potential condition (the so-called future less vivid) with εἰ plus the optative in the protasis and the optative plus ἄν in the apodosis. Sm. §2329. It considers the possibility of an event, without expecting it to come true. But then there is another qualifying protasis, a real protasis with future indicative, introduced by εἴπερ, meaning "if indeed, if in fact," which signals that the condition is unfavorable or to be feared. Sm. §§2328, 2328a.

The backbone of this sentence follows.

εἰ ἄρξαιτε
   μεταβάλοιτε ἂν τὴν εὐνοίαν
      ἣν εἰλήφατε

εἴπερ γνώσεσθε ὁμοῖα
    οἷα ὑπεδείξατε

ἄν is repeated, as in Thuc. I.76.4. Sm. §1765.

τὸ ἡμέτερον δέος. "fear of us." The possessive pronominal adjective stands for the objective genitive. Sm. §§1331, 1334.

The sentence may be translated,

So if you should destroy us and take over our empire, you would quickly lose the goodwill you have gained because we were feared . . .

πρὸς τὸν Μῆδον δι' ὀλίγου ἡγησάμενοι. "when for a short time you were in leadership against the Mede."

γνώσεσθε. ὁμοῖα γιγνώσκειν means "to have similar attitudes and principles of action." The definition in LSJ (s.v. γιγνώσκω II.1), "form a judgement, think," does not adequately treat this pregnant meaning. γνώσεσθε is middle merely because the future of γιγνώσκω is deponent γνώσομαι. Hence, "if, in fact, you are going to maintain a policy similar to that which you demonstrated when for a time you led against the Mede."

ἄμεικτα. Neuter plural verbal adjective from μείγνυμι, "mix"—hence, "unmixed." LSJ spells the word ἄμικτος. It is used of cultural monsters— e.g., centaurs and Cyclopes—who are savage and socially incompatible. Here, it means that the Spartan customs are "incompatible, and inharmonious with the customs and manners of others, and therefore not conducive to sincere and candid intercourse" (Classen and Steup, ad loc.).

78.1. βουλεύεσθε is an imperative and is parallel with the aorist subjunctive πρόσθησθε with negative μή, which is a negative command or prohibitive subjunctive. Sm. §1800.

ὡς οὐ περὶ βραχέων. "since it does not concern trifles." This is a litotes meaning "since it concerns weighty matters." LSJ s.v. βραχύς 4.

78.2. φιλεῖ. Thucydides uses the verb φιλέω only in the meaning "be used to, be accustomed to, customarily do" (LSJ s.v. II) and usually with an infinitive. The subject is ὁ πόλεμος.

τὰ πολλά. Adverbial.

περιίστασθαι. When used of events, περιίστημι means "turn out, come around to, depend on." LSJ s.v. B.II.3 (middle).

ὧν ἴσον ἀπέχομεν. The antecedent of ὧν is τυχάς. ἴσον is adverbial, meaning "equally." ἀπέχομεν means "be away from" and takes the genitive of the place (or event). LSJ s.v. ἀπέχω III. Hence, "chances from which we are equally removed." The phrase means that neither side in a war has control over the accidents.

ἐν ἀδήλῳ κινδυνεύεται. "The risk is taken in uncertainty [of the outcome]." LSJ s.v. ἄδηλος II.1b.

78.3. τῶν ἔργων πρότερον ἔχονται. "They grasp at actions first." LSJ s.v. ἔχω C.I.2 (middle with genitive).

κακοπαθοῦντες δὲ ἤδη. "but once they are already in trouble." ἤδη goes with the participle. Sm. §2080.

78.4. ἕως ἔτι with the indicative (here, the missing verb ἐστί) means "so long as still." Sm. §2422. Hence, "as long as we both still have [the opportunity of] sound and independent counsel."

μὴ λύειν, μηδὲ παραβαίνειν, and λύεσθαι are indirect imperatives after the leading verb λέγομεν. Smyth treats this construction under the usage of verbs of will and desire. Sm. §1997; see also §2633.

ταύτῃ ᾗ ἂν ὑφηγῆσθε. "in this direction wherever you may lead."

80.1. ἐν τῇ αὐτῇ ἡλικίᾳ. "of the same age as myself."

τινα. Masculine singular accusative of the indefinite pronoun, meaning "anyone [of you older men]," used as the subject of the infinitive.

τοῦ ἔργου. τὸ ἔργον, here the genitive object of ἐπιθυμῆσαι, is frequently used to refer to the deeds of war and fighting. LSJ s.v. I.1. Since this is a common Homeric usage, perhaps Thucydides has lent something of an epic flavor to the speech of Archidamus.

80.3. παρόμοιος ἡμῶν ἡ ἀλκή. παρόμοιος is a feminine two-ending adjective because it is compound. Sm. §288. ἀλκή is an epic and poetic word meaning "strength, prowess, courage, effectiveness of defense." Hence, "our strength was comparable."

ἐφ᾽ ἕκαστα. When used of military aims, this construction means "against each objective."

πόλεμον ἄρασθαι. Here, the aorist middle infinitive of ἀείρω is transitive and means "undertake." LSJ s.v. IV.4. The subject of the infinitive is an understood ἡμᾶς, implied in the accusative plural participle πιστεύσαντας.

ἐπειχθῆναι. Aorist passive infinitive of ἐπείγω, "press, drive, urge," which in the passive means "hasten, hurry, be in a hurry." LSJ s.v. III.3.

80.4. πότερον ταῖς ναυσίν; This picks up the rhetorical question πῶς; hence, "Is it by means of ships?" πότερον introduces direct alternative questions. Sm. §2656.

εἰ μελετήσομεν . . . ἐνέσται. Real condition with futures, in which the simple logical connection between the clauses is emphasized. This is not what Smyth calls the "emotional future" (Sm. §2328) but merely a real (or "logical") condition in the future. Cf. Sm. §2301; Kühner-Gerth 2:466, §573. Hence, "if we really are going to prepare . . . , it will take time."

ἀλλὰ τοῖς χρήμασιν; We would expect ἤ to mark the second of the direct alternative questions. But we have here the figure called *hypophora*. Sm. §3029. Denniston (*Gr. Part.*², 10–11) says, "The proferring and rejecting of successive suggestions may be done by a single speaker, who conducts, as it were, a dialogue with himself. This device, known as hypophora, is freely used, for liveliness and variety by the Greek orators." Cf. Thuc. VI.38.5.

ἔχομεν . . . φέρομεν. The direct object of these verbs, understood from the preceding, is χρήματα.

αὐτῶν is not a possessive with ὅπλοις but a genitive with ὑπερφέρομεν— hence, "we surpass them."

81.3. εἰ . . . πειράσομεθα . . . δεήσει. Real condition with futures. Sm. §2301.

81.5. ἄλλως τε καί. "especially." Sm. §2980.

81.6. εἰκός. "It is likely that . . ." (plus an infinitive). "εἰκός regularly takes the aorist infinitive (never future), where the probability of the occurrence of a future action is to be expressed" (Classen and Steup, ad loc.). Sm. §1868b.

82.1. Οὐ μὴν οὐδὲ κτλ. This complicated sentence has only two main verbs, the indicative κελεύω and the hortatory subjunctive ἐκποριζώμεθα, both expressions of bidding and desire. They are connected by the καὶ that introduces the ἐκποριζώμεθα clause. κελεύω, meaning "bid," introduces seven infinitives that represent indirect imperatives, ἐᾶν, μὴ καταφωρᾶν, μήπω κινεῖν, πέμπειν, αἰτιᾶσθαι, ἐξαρτύεσθαι. Smyth does not call them indirect imperatives but treats them under verbs of will and desire. Sm. §§1991–92. The understood subject accusative of these infinitives is ὑμᾶς, but it is omitted because it is already clear to whom Archidamus is speaking. Sm. §1972.

Οὐ μὴν οὐδὲ. "nor again surely not." Sm. §§2768, 2921.

ἀναισθήτως. "with indifference."

αὐτοὺς κελεύω . . . καταφωρᾶν. αὐτοὺς refers to the Athenians. A re-arrangement of the sentence follows.

> ουδὲ κελεύω (ὑμᾶς) ἐᾶν αὐτοὺς βλάπτειν τοὺς συμμάχους ουδὲ κελεύω (ὑμᾶς) μὴ καταφωρᾶν (αὐτοὺς) ἐπιβουλεύοντας ἀλλά . . . μήπω κινεῖν.

> [I do not suggest you should allow them to injure the allies, nor do I suggest you should not catch them red-handed when they are plotting intrigues, but I do suggest . . ."]

In my translation, English *should* is not potential but, rather, marks an indirect imperative. ἀλλὰ neutralizes the negatives, and κελεύω becomes positive.

αἰτιᾶσθαι μήτε . . . δηλοῦντας μήθ᾽ ὡς ἐπιτρέψομεν. αἰτιᾶσθαι is used absolutely to mean "make your complaints." δηλοῦντας agrees with the omitted subject ὑμᾶς, and the negatives are μὴ because they are still under the regimen of the indirect imperatives after κελεύω. Hence, "without suggesting [literally, "making clear"] war." μήθ᾽ ὡς ἐπιτρέψομεν is logically, though not grammatically, parallel. Hence, "nor as if we are about to give in."

κἂν τούτῳ = καὶ ἐν τούτῳ. Temporal, meaning "and in this period of time, in this interval."

τὰ ἡμέτερ᾽ αὐτῶν. "our own resources." αὐτῶν modifies τὰ ἡμέτερα by a *constructio ad sensum.* Sm. §§1200.2b, 1203b, 1203b.N.

εἰ . . . προσληψόμεθα is not really a condition but an "in case" clause, or according to Smyth's categorization, an "on the chance that" clause. Sm. §2354.

ἀνεπίφθονον . . . διασωθῆναι. The infinitive διασωθῆναι is the subject, and the neuter adjective ἀνεπίφθονον is the predicate adjective. The infinitive has an accusative subject, προσλαβόντας, which is modified by the relative clause. Hence, "it is not invidious for those who are being plotted against to find safety by enlisting the aid of both Greeks and barbarians."

ἐπιβουλευόμεθα. Instead of the expected third plural ἐπιβουεύλονται, the verb is attracted to the first person by ὥσπερ ἡμεῖς.

τὰ αὐτῶν = τὰ ἡμέτερα αὐτῶν. This is somewhat awkward, and some editors have proposed τὰ αὐτοῦ, "things here."

82.2. ἢν δὲ μὴ . . . ἴμεν. Eventual condition with ἐάν plus the subjunctive (omitted—it would have been ἐσακούωσι) in the protasis and a future indicative (ἴμεν) in the apodosis (the so-called future more vivid). Sm. §§2323, 2326a. ἴμεν (*ibimus*) has future force.

82.3. τοὺς λόγους αὐτῇ ὁμοῖα ὑποσημαίνοντας. αὐτῇ refers to παρασκευήν and is dative after ὁμοῖα. Hence, "pronouncements hinting at things corresponding to our preparation."

82.4. μὴ . . . νομίσητε. Prohibitive subjunctive aorist. Sm. §1800.

ὅσῳ ἄμεινον ἐξείργασται. "the better it is cultivated."

ἧς φείδεσθαι χρή. I.e., it is necessary for the Spartans to spare the Athenian land, which they consider as a hostage.

ἀληπτοτέρους ἔχειν. "find them more difficult to deal with." ἀληπτοτέρους is a comparative verbal adjective from λαμβάνω with alpha privative. Cf. Thuc. I.37, 143.

82.5. ὁρᾶτε ὅπως μὴ . . . πράξομεν. ὅπως μή plus the future after a verb of effort (ὁρᾶτε). Hence, "See to it that we do not do something worse."

ὁράω serves as a verb of effort only with negative clauses. Sm. §§2209, 2210b, 2211.

82.6. οἷόν τε = οἷόν τ᾽ ἐστι. "it is possible." ἐστί is often omitted in this idiom.

καθ᾽ ὅτι χωρήσει. "how it will come out"—literally, "according to what it will come out." κατά indicates manner. Sm. §1690.2c.

πόλεμον . . . θέσθαι. "to settle a war suitably." LSJ s.v. τίθημι VII.1.Med. Cf. Thuc. I.25.1.

83.2. ὅπλων . . . δαπάνης. "Pregnant genitives" dependent on εἶναι— hence, "about weapons . . . money." These are predicate genitives acting like predicate adjectives. Smyth calls them "genitives of quality." Sm. §1320. Here, the word δαπάνη means "financial resources."

τὸ πλέον. Thucydides often uses τὸ πλέον instead of μᾶλλον. Sm. §1068.

ὠφελεῖ here means "be effective"—for someone, in the dative (ἠπειρώ-ταις), against someone, in the accusative with πρός (πρὸς θαλασσίους).

83.3. αὐτήν. I.e., δαπάνην.

πορισώμεθα . . . ἐπαιρώμεθα. Hortatory subjunctives. Sm. §1797. LSJ s.v. ἐπαίρω II ("get excited, be carried away").

τῶν ἀποβαινόντων. "the consequences, things that follow."

τὸ πλέον is here the object of ἕξομεν with the genitive τῆς αἰτίας. Hence, "the greater part of the blame for the consequences."

οὗτοι. οὗτος is used instead of ὅς to avoid the repetition of the relative. Sm. §2517.

ἐπ᾽ ἀμφότερα. "whichever way things turn out"—literally, "toward both things." LSJ s.v. ἐπί C.I.3 ("of the quarter or direction towards or in which a thing takes place").

84.1. σπεύδοντές τε is picked up by καὶ . . . νεμόμεθα. σπεύδοντές is a conditional participle. Sm. §2067.

σχολαίτερον ἂν παύσαισθε. "You would more slowly cease." In the ac-tive, παύω is transitive and means "stop or hinder something." In the middle, it is intransitive and means "stop doing something," and it very often occurs with a supplementary participle (e.g., παύομαι λέγων, "I stop speaking"). Sm. §2098. Without such a participle, it has the simple intransitive meaning "stop, cease, make an end." LSJ s.v. I.3.

ἀπαράσκευοι. This subject of the articular infinitive is nominative (rather than accusative) because it refers to the subject of the leading verb. Sm. §1973a.

84.2. εὐπραγίαις οὐκ ἐξυβρίζομεν. "We do not get puffed up with successes."

τῶν ἐξοτρυνόντων is dependent on ἡδόνῃ. ἐπὶ τὰ δεινά after ἐξοτρυνόντων ἡμᾶς means "toward risky enterprises."

παρὰ τὸ δοκοῦν ἡμῖν. "contrary to our judgment"—literally, "contrary to what seems good to us." δοκοῦν is the neuter participle of δοκέω.

ἀνεπείσθημεν. Aorist in the apodosis of a present general condition. The gnomic aorist (Sm. §1931) is equivalent here to a present indicative. Sm. §§1931a, 2338.

84.3. πολεμικοὶ . . . διαιρετάς. This complicated sentence has only one main verb, γιγνόμεθα, and the rest depends on nominative participles and adjectives, which govern further dependent constructions. The whole sentence explains what Archidamus means by πολεμικοί, on the one hand, and εὔβουλοι, on the other; the first point is short, and the second point is greatly expanded.

The backbone of this sentence and a rough preliminary translation follows.

γιγνόμεθα
   πολεμικοὶ
      τὸ **μὲν** ὅτι
         αἰδὼς μετέχει σωφροσύνης πλεῖστον
         εὐψυχία δὲ (μετέχει) αἰσχύνης (πλεῖστον)
   εὔβουλοι **δὲ**
      παιδευόμενοι
         ἀμαθέστερον (plus the genitive τῆς ὑπεροψίας)
         καὶ σωφρονέστερον ἢ ὥστε ἀνηκούστειν
         καὶ . . . μὴ ἐπεξιέναι
         νομίζειν δὲ

[We are warlike because honor is the greatest part of prudence and [because] courage is the greatest part of honor; and we are wise because we are educated less learnedly than to disdain the laws, [educated] more wisely than to ignore them, [educated] not to attack, but [educated] to consider.]

αἰδώς and αἰσχύνη are here synonymous; both mean something like "the sense of honor." The participle παιδευόμενοι is causal and is parallel to the two ὅτι clauses. The four parallel constructions after παιδευόμενοι need further analysis.

ἀμαθέστερον τῶν νόμων τῆς ὑπεροψίας παιδευόμενοι. The adverb is ironic. Hence, "we are educated less learnedly than to disdain the laws," i.e., "we are not so sophisticated as to despise the laws." Archidamus, picking up on the charge that the Spartans are not elegantly educated, turns it around by making that a virtue.

καὶ ξὺν χαλεπότητι σωφρονέστερον ἢ ὥστε αὐτῶν ἀνηκουστεῖν (παιδευόμενοι). ξὺν χαλεπότητι means "with severe discipline." LSJ s.v. χαλεπότης II. ὥστε . . . ἀνηκουστεῖν expresses the anticipated or possible result (not the actual result). Sm. §2260. Hence, "we are educated—with severe discipline—with more self-control than to pay no heed to them [the laws]."

καὶ μὴ τὰ ἀχρεῖα . . . ἐπεξιέναι (παιδευόμενοι). The basic construction is παιδευόμενοι μὴ ἐπεξιέναι (τοῖς πολεμίοις) [educated not to go against [the enemies]]. There is some dispute among commentators and translators about the construction of ἐπεξιέναι. Thucydides treats it as intransitive without complement at II.21 but with a dative at VI.97, and the latter seems to be the construction here. The negative μή goes with the infinitive, not the participles—hence, "we have learned not to . . ."

ὄντες and μεμφόμενοι are two dependent participles connected by apposition. The participle μεμφόμενοι gives an example of what is meant by being too clever. Sm. §2147g.

τὰ ἀχρεῖα ξυνετοὶ ἄγαν ὄντες. "being too clever with respect to useless things"—e.g., making a fine theoretical assessment of the enemy's preparations.

The contrast between λόγος and ἔργον marks the connection between the participle μεμφόμενοι and the infinitive ἐπεξιέναι. Hence, "while cleverly criticizing in talk the enemies' plans, not to go after them in fact in a manner inconsistent [with the words]."

νομίζειν δὲ . . . διαιϱέτας. "but [we are educated] to think that the plans and calculations of others are comparable to our own and [to think] that accidents that happen by chance cannot be determined by calculation." οἱ πέλας literally means "those nearby," but in Thucydides it usually means simply "others." Classen and Steup, at I.32.1.

85.1. μὴ παϱῶμεν. Negative hortatory subjunctive with first plural aorist active of παϱίημι, "give up, abandon." LSJ s.v. III.1.

ἡμῖν μᾶλλον ἑτέϱων. "for us more than [for] others."

85.2. ἑτοίμων ὄντων. I.e., the Athenians.

δίκας δοῦναι. "submit to arbitration."

86.2. οἱ δ' οὐκέτι μέλλουσι. I.e., the allies. Sthenelaidas seems to be making a witty remark: "We will not put off helping. They don't put off suffering!" For additional examples of Laconic humor, see Plutarch's *Apothegmata Laconica* (*Mor.* 208B–236E).

86.3. παϱαδοτέα. For the neuter plural, see Sm. §§1052, 1003a. The impersonal construction of the verbal in ‾τέος takes an accusative object. Sm. §2152.

μὴ λόγῳ αὐτοὺς βλαπτομένους. The accusative participle has the negative μή because it is conditional. Sm. §§2067, 2728. It is the agent of the verbal διακριτέα. "Since the impersonal construction is virtually active, and hence equivalent to δεῖ with the accusative and infinitive . . . , the agent sometimes stands in the accusative" (Sm. §2152a). ἡμᾶς is to be supplied.

The sentence may be translated, "Decision by means of arbitration and words must not be made by us, if we ourselves are not being harmed by words"—i.e., "if it is not by words that we are being harmed."

87.2. ἀναστήτω. Root aorist active third singular imperative.

87.6. προκεχωρηκυιῶν. Genitive feminine plural perfect active participle of προχωρέω, "proceed, go well." Hence, "[the truce] having gone well, succeeded [until this fourteenth year]." LSJ s.v. II.1.

89.3. Ἀθηναίων τὸ κοινόν. "the Athenian people." This expression takes plural verbs by *constructio ad sensum*. Sm. §950.

διεκομίζοντο is transitive, with the objects παῖδας and γυναῖκας. The clause ὅθεν ὑπεξέθεντο is somewhat condensed for ἐντεῦθεν οἷ ὑπεξέθεντο αὐτούς.

90.1. τὸ μέλλον. Object of αἰσθανόμενοι—hence, "what was about to happen."

τὰ μὲν . . . τὸ δὲ πλέον. Adverbial, meaning "on the one hand . . . , but more . . ."

ἥδιον ἂν ὁρῶντες . . . μηδένα . . . ἔχοντα. ἔχοντα is a participle in indirect discourse after a verb of perceiving (ὁρῶντες). Sm. §§2110–12. ὁρῶντες is a causal participle, giving one of the reasons for sending the embassy. Sm. §2064. ἂν indicates an original potential optative (Sm. §§1845–46), which would have been ἥδιον ἂν ὁρῷμεν, "we would prefer to see." Hence, "on the grounds that they would prefer to see no one having . . ." The negatives μήτε . . . μήτε . . . μηδένα are something of a puzzle. Ordinarily, the participle in indirect discourse after a verb of perceiving would take οὐ. Sm. §2608. But here, we have a case of a wish that the utterance would hold good. If this were a construction of verb of saying plus the infinitive involving the wish that the utterance would hold good, the negative of the infinitive in indirect discourse would be μή. Sm. §2723. By analogy, when the leading verb (here, ὁράω) takes a participle, the negative will be μή. Sm. §2608.

ὁρῶντες . . . ἐξοτρυνόντων. By Thucydides' usual stylistic habit of off-target parallelism, the nominative participle is balanced by the genitive absolute to express the two causes.

90.2. ξυγκαθελεῖν μετὰ σφῶν. "to join with them [the Spartans] in tearing down the surrounding walls."

τῶν ἔξω Πελοποννήσου. "of the people outside the Peloponnese."

ὅσοις εἱστήκει (τὰ τείχη). "whose [walls] were still standing." The relative ὅσος is used to emphasize the number ("however so many"). It is dative of possession. The pluperfect εἱστήκει marks the past of a continuing condition; i.e., ἕστηκα, "stand," is a perfect with present meaning (Sm. §1946), and its pluperfect, εἱστήκει, has corresponding imperfect meaning.

τὸ μὲν βουλόμενον καὶ ὕποπτον τῆς γνώμης. Neuter adjective for abstract noun (the *schema Thucydideum*). Hence, "the intention and suspicion [that lay behind] the opinion."

ὡς δὲ τοῦ βαρβάρου . . . οὐκ ἂν ἔχοντος. ὡς with the genitive absolute indicating the ground of belief. Sm. §2086d. οὐκ ἂν ἔχοντος represents an original potential optative. Sm. §§1845–46. It really represents the apodosis of a potential condition, whose protasis is the clause εἰ ἐπέλθοι.

90.3. ἀπήλλαξαν. "got rid of, dismissed." LSJ s.v. ἀπαλλάσσω A.I.3.

90.4. ὑπεῖπον is an aorist that lacks a corresponding present. As a substitute, the suppletive verb ὑπαγορεύω is used for its present (instead of ὑπολέγω, which does not occur until the Roman period). Here, it means "add, subjoin, say in addition." LSJ s.v. 3.

90.5. ὁπότε . . . ἔροιτο. General temporal clause ("whenever" clause) in secondary sequence. The primary form ὁπόταν ἔρωται loses its ἄν and becomes optative. Sm. §§2410, 2414. Smyth's treatment of general temporal clauses is confusing and unclear. They behave exactly like eventual conditions ("if ever" conditions) and general relative clauses ("whoever" clauses) with the subjunctive plus ἄν in primary sequence and the optative without ἄν in secondary sequence.

91.1. οὐκ εἶχον ὅπως χρὴ ἀπιστῆσαι. Literally, "They had not how it was necessary to disbelieve." The nominal ὅπως clause is the direct object of εἶχον. οὐκ ἔχω here means "be unable to, not know how to." LSJ s.v. ἔχω A.III.2. Warner translates, "They did not see how they could reject such information."

91.3. ἐφοβεῖτο . . . μὴ . . . οὐκέτι ἀφῶσιν. Clause of fearing. Sm. §§2221, 2225. The negative μὴ . . . οὐ is used to express fear that something may not happen. The sequence is secondary after ἐφοβεῖτο, and the eventual "whenever" clause ὁπότε . . . ἀκούσειαν is optative for that reason. But why is ἀφῶσιν, the third plural aorist active subjunctive of ἀφίημι, not changed to the optative? "After secondary tenses, the subjunctive presents the fear vividly, *i.e.* as it was conceived by the subject. . . . The vivid use of subjunctive is common in the historians, especially Thucydides" (Sm. §2226).

91.4. ἰέναι. Indirect imperative. Hence, "He said that they should go . . ." Sm. §§2633c, 1997.

91.5. ὅσα . . . βουλεύεσθαι. The verb in the relative clause is attracted into the infinitive by the running indirect discourse. Sm. §2631. This relative clause serves as an accusative of respect with οὐδένος ὕστεροι. Hence, "With respect to whatever they had deliberated with them, they [the Athenians] appeared second to none in judgment."

91.6. ἰδίᾳ. Adverb. LSJ s.v. ἴδιος VI.2. Hence, "in particular, privately."

91.7. ἔφη χρῆναι . . . ἢ καὶ τάδε νομίζειν ὀρθῶς ἔχειν. "he said it was necessary . . . to consider that these things [i.e., building the walls] were right."

92.1. οὐδὲ γὰρ ἐπὶ κωλύμῃ, ἀλλὰ γνώμης παραινέσει. "not for the purpose of prevention, but for the purpose of recommending a policy." LSJ s.v. ἐπί B.III.2.

ἀνεπικλήτως. "without preferring any charge, without complaint."

93.2. οὐ ξυνειργασμένων ἔστιν ᾗ. The fixed phrase ἔστιν ᾗ is adverbial and acts like a single adverb meaning "in some way, somehow, anyhow." Sm. §2515. Hence, "not fitted together in any way."

πάντα ὁμοίως κινοῦντες ἠπείγοντο. ἐπείγω means "hasten, hurry." LSJ s.v. III.3. Because the simple verb (*εἴγω) does not occur, ἐπείγω is not treated as a compound, and the augment goes onto the preverb. Sm. §450. κινέω means "remove a thing from its place, disturb" and can be used of meddling with things that should be left alone. LSJ s.v. I.2. Hence, "they disturbed everything indiscriminately in their haste."

93.4. ἀνθεκτέα. Neuter plural nominative verbal adjective from ἀντέχω, which takes the genitive when it means "hold on to." LSJ s.v. III.2. The full-grade root of this verb is *segh- >*σεχ⁻ >ἐχ⁻. Hence, in the verbal, the initial rough breathing shows up, as it does in the verbal adjective in *-tos—e.g., in the compound καθεκτός, "checked, held back." Because the χ is assimilated to the τ, giving κ, Grassmann's Law (dissimilation of aspirates) does not operate. The neuter plural of the verbal is often used in the impersonal construction. Sm. §2152; cf. §1052. Hence, "that the sea must be held on to."

93.5. δύο ἅμαξαι. There is some argument about what this means. This sentence must somehow pertain to the width of the wall. Gomme (ad loc.) sees no difficulty: "There is no difficulty here either in the meaning or in the expression of it: two wagons, going in opposite directions, brought the stones up on to the wall (and, of course, passed each other; the wall would have had to be yet wider, if they were compelled to turn)."

93.6. ἀφιστᾶναι τὰς . . . ἐπιβουλάς. "fend off the attacks."

ἀρκέσειν. "will be enough, suffice" (intransitive). LSJ s.v. ἀρκέω III.4.

93.7. προσέκειτο. "be devoted to, concentrate on" (plus the dative). LSJ s.v. πρόσκειμαι II.2.

94.1. ἐν τῇδε τῇ ἡγεμονίᾳ. Temporal, meaning "during this period of command."

95.1. The adjective βίαιος, referring to Pausanias, means "arrogant, dictatorial, violent." In the middle, the verb βιάζομαι means "act violently or dictatorially."

95.2. προσεῖχον τὴν γνώμην is like the expression προσέχειν τὸν νοῦν, "pay attention, give heed to." LSJ s.v. προσέχω I.3. With the object γνώμην, the phrase means "be determined."

ὡς οὐ περιοψόμενοι τἆλλά τε καταστησόμενοι. ὡς plus the future participle giving the ground of Athenian determination. Sm. §2086. Since there is a future participle, there is also an element of purpose here. Sm. §2065. οὐ περιοψόμενοι is for οὐ περιοψόμενοι ἢν βιάζηται and is a future-more-vivid condition downgraded to a participle. Originally, it would be ἢν βιάζηται, οὐ περιοψόμεθα, "If ever he gets rough, we will not overlook it." τε makes clear that τἆλλα is the object of καταστησόμενοι.

95.4. ξυνέβη takes two infinitive phrases connected by τε . . . τε: "It happened to him to be recalled" [αὐτῷ καλεῖσθαι] and, at the same time, "it happened that the allies changed sides [μετατάξασθαι]."

95.5. τῶν ἀδικημάτων. Genitive of the charge—Smyth's genitive of crime and accountability. Sm. §1375.

τὰ μέγιστα. Internal accusative object of ἀδικεῖν.

μὴ ἀδικεῖν. A verb of negative meaning (here, ἀπολύω, "acquit") can take the infinitive with μὴ. Sm. §§2739–40.

95.7. οἱ δὲ αἰσθανόμενοι. δέ changes the subject, now the Spartans. αἰσθανόμενοι has no explicit object but refers to what has just been said.

ἀπαλλαξείοντες. ἀπαλλαξείω is the desiderative of ἀπαλλάσσω. Sm. §868.

ἐπιτηδείους. "friendly." LSJ s.v. II.2.

ἔταξαν ἅς τε ἔδει παρέχειν τῶν πόλεων χρήματα πρὸς τὸν βάρβαρον καὶ ἅς ναῦς. The relative pronouns serve here as indirect interrogatives. Sm. §§339f, 2668. Hence, "They settled which cities were obliged . . ."

96.2. Ἑλληνοταμίαι . . . ἀρχή. "The office of Hellenotamiai was set up." ἀρχή is appositive to Ἑλληνοταμίαι. On the assessment of the tribute by Aristides, see [Arist.] *Ath. Pol.* 23.4–5 and Thuc. V.18.5.

97.1. τοσάδε ἐπῆλθον. τοσάδε means "the several points to follow." τόσος is the demonstrative that emphasizes quantity or number. Sm. §340. Hence, "they turned to the following series of enterprises." ἐπέρχομαι means "accomplish." LSJ s.v. III.3. The datives πολέμῳ and διαχειρίσει are datives of means (Sm. §1506 ff.)—hence, "by means of warfare and the energetic management of affairs."

ἃ ἐγένετο αὐτοῖς. The antecedent of the relative is τοσάδε. The dative αὐτοῖς is a remnant of the idiom πόλεμος ἐγένετο πρὸς τούτους αὐτοῖς. Cf. Thuc. I.98.

προστυγχάνοντας ἐν ἑκάστῳ. "those who in each case came in contact with them."

97.2. τὴν ἐκβολὴν τοῦ λόγου. "the digression from the narrative," i.e., the Pentecontaetia.

τὸ χωρίον. "subject area." LSJ s.v. 6b. Others translate, "period of time, part or circumstance." Crawley translates, "passage of history." Warner translates, "period."

Ἀττικὴ Συγγραφή is the title of Hellanicus's work.

ἔχει = παρέχει. "provides, supplies." The missing subject is ἡ ἐκβόλη.

98.4. παρὰ τὸ καθεστηκός. "contrary to the established [constitution of the Delian League]."

ὡς ἑκάστῃ is feminine because it refers to ξυμμαχίς, which is here dative with ξυνέβη. The ὡς is a problem. Classen and Steup (ad loc.) expand this brachylogy (Sm. §3017) as καὶ τῶν ἄλλων ἑκάστη ἐδουλώθη ὡς ἑκάστῃ ξυνέβη δουλωθῆναι [and each of the others was enslaved as it happened to each one to be enslaved]. They explain that this refers to the fact that differing circumstances led to enslavement in each case. Hence, "then the others were enslaved for various reasons." Warner translates, "and the process was continued in the cases of the other allies as various circumstances arose."

99.1. ἔκδειαι. "defaults in tribute and contributions of ships."

λιποστρατίον. Gomme (ad loc.) explains, "λιποστρατίον here must mean something distinct from νεῶν ἔκδειαι, and implies therefore 'return home in the middle of a campaign'; not on the part of individual men or regiments or crews, but of whole contingents, recalled by their authorities."

εἴ τῳ ἐγένετο. Real condition in the past, with a hint of generality. Smyth calls this "the indicative form of general conditions" (Sm. §2342). Its generality is signaled by the indefinite pronoun. Cf. εἴ τίς τι ἐπηρώτα, ἀπεκρίναντο [If ever anybody asked anything, they answered] (Thuc. 7.10). Hence, here, "if ever it happened to anyone." It refers to λιποστρατίον alone, and Gomme translates, "occasional desertion."

προσάγοντες τὰς ἀνάγκας. "by applying coercive measures." Crawley translates, "by applying the screw of necessity." Warner translates, "by bringing the severest pressure to bear."

99.2. πως καὶ ἄλλως. "in some other respects, in other ways."

προσάγεσθαι . . . αὐτοῖς τοὺς ἀφισταμένους. "reduce to subjection to them any who revolted."

99.3. τὴν ἀπόκνησιν τῶν στρατειῶν. "the shrinking from military expeditions."

ἵνα . . . ὦσι. Purpose clause that did not change to optative after a past verb. Sm. §2197. Thucydides prefers this "vivid subjunctive."

ἢν ἐκεῖνοι ξυμφέροιεν. General relative clause in secondary sequence. The primary form would be ἢν ἂν ἐκεῖνοι ξυμφέρωσι. Sm. §§2567–68.

ὁπότε ἀποσταῖεν. General temporal clause in secondary sequence. The primary form would be ὁπόταν ἀποστῶσι. Sm. §§2409, 2414.

πολέμιον ἦν τὸ χωρίον κτιζόμενον. "The settlement of the place was regarded with hostility." This construction, by which the attributive participle and its noun correspond to a verbal abstract noun plus a genitive (Sm. §2053), is traditionally known by its designation in Latin grammar as the *ab urbe condita* construction. Cf. Thuc. III.29.2: ἡμέραι μάλιστα ἦσαν τῇ Μιτυλήνῃ ἑαλωκυῖα ἑπτά [It was about seven days since the capture of Mitylene].

102.2. τοῖς δὲ . . . τούτου ἐνδεᾶ ἐφαίνετο. τοῖς δέ refers to the Spartans and serves both as the dative after ἐφαίνετο and as a dative with ἐνδεᾶ, which is a neuter plural adjective taking the genitive of what is lacking and the dative of the person(s) to whom it is lacking, used in place of the abstract noun ἔνδεια. Hence, "It seemed to the Spartans that they lacked this [i.e., τειχομάχειν]." Some editors argue that τοῖς δέ refers to the Athenians and means that the Athenians fell short of their reputation.

102.3. ἅμα ἀμφοτέροις. "with both parties"; i.e., both the Athenians and the Argives made an alliance with the Thessalians.

103.1. ἐφ᾽ ᾧ. "on the condition that." LSJ s.v. ἐπί B.III.3. This is a clause of proviso with future indicative (favored by Thucydides), which takes negative μή. Sm. §2279. The verb εἶμι has future force. Sm. §1880.

εἶναι. The direct form of this condition would be ἢν ἁλίσκηται . . . ἔστω δοῦλος; i.e., it is an eventual condition downgraded to an infinitive phrase. There are two possible explanations for the infinitive construction. It may continue the proviso, but changing the construction from ἐφ᾽ ᾧ with the future to ἐφ᾽ ᾧ with the infinitive. Sm. §2279. Hence, "on the condition that if anyone is caught, he is to be a slave." Or the infinitive may be dependent on ξυνέβησαν (Classen-Steup). Hence, "They agreed that if . . ."

103.2. τοῦ Ἰθωμήτα. Ἰθωμήτα is the genitive of a masculine a-stem noun (like μαθήτης). Masculine a-stem nouns have taken on the genitive ending of o-stem nouns by analogy. In Attic, the ending is framed to rhyme with the o-stem nouns (e.g., μαθήτου). But in other dialects, such as Doric, the genitive ending ⁻ο (from ⁻οιο) is added to the stem-formative ⁻α⁻, yielding *Ἰθωμήτα⁻ο, which becomes by vowel contraction Ἰθωμ-ήτᾱ. Buck, *Comp. Gr.*, §236.3. Thucydides uses the Doric form.

104.1. ἐπηγάγετο. "brought in as allies." LSJ s.v. ἐπάγω II.2.

105.3. ἢν δὲ καὶ βοητῶσιν . . . ἀναστήσεσθαι. Eventual condition with future apodosis (future more vivid) in indirect discourse after νομίζοντες. The leading verb is κατέβησαν, but the conditional clause does not change to secondary sequence. Sm. §2599, 2619.

106.2. γνόντες. I.e., the Athenians were familiar with the place.

κατὰ πρόσωπόν τε εἶργον (αὐτούς) τοῖς ὁπλίταις. "hemmed them in in front by means of the hoplites." LSJ s.v. πρόσωπον I.1. The hoplites are in the dative because, despite the fact that they are persons, they are here regarded as instruments. Sm. §1507b.

τοὺς ψιλούς is the object of the transitive sigmatic aorist περιστήσαντες.

107.3. εἰ βούλοιντο . . . ἔμελλον κωλύσειν. In primary sequence, this condition would have the form ἐὰν βούλωνται . . . μέλλουσι κωλύσειν, "If ever they want to . . . , the Athenians are going to prevent . . ." It is an eventual condition with future apodosis (future more vivid), with the peculiarity that the apodosis has μέλλω plus a future infinitive, rather than simple future. The future is put into the past by the use of the imperfect μέλλω—hence, "they were going to." Then, with the past leading verb, the "if" clause goes into the optative and loses its ἄν. Hence, "If ever they wanted to . . . , the Athenians were going to prevent . . ." Smyth calls such constructions "past general conditions" (Sm. §2340) but does not treat the special case with μέλλω. He treats the imperfect of μέλλω only as a substitute for the potential aorist. Sm. §§1960, 2328.

107.4. τὸ δέ τι is a fixed phrase functioning as an adverb meaning "partly." The point is that there were some Athenians, a party within the city, who were secretly trying to encourage the Spartans. LSJ s.v. ἐπάγω. I.4. ἐπῆγον is a conative imperfect. Sm. §1895.

107.5. ὡς ἕκαστοι. "each for himself." Sm. §2997.

107.6. ἀπορεῖν. The subject of this infinitive would be the Spartans. "When the subject of the infinitive is the same as the *object* (in the genitive or dative [here, αὐτοῖς]) of the governing verb [here, ἐπεστράτευσαν], it is often omitted" (Sm. §1978). Hence, "[The Athenians] thinking that [the Spartans] were at a loss in what direction to make their escape, [the Athenians] attacked them [the Spartans]." διέλθωσιν is subjunctive because it represents a deliberative subjunctive embedded in an indirect question.

καί τι καί. The first καί is copulative, the second adverbial. The first καί marks an addition to the preceding, the second the fact that the addition is surprising. Denniston, *Gr. Part.*², 294. Hence, "and even somewhat because of the suspicion . . ."

108.5. ἐν ἀποβάσει τῆς γῆς. "in an amphibious landing"—i.e., landing from ships.

109.1. ἰδέαι. "kinds, forms, sorts." LSJ s.v. I.3.

109.2. ὅπως . . . ἀπαγάγοι. Purpose clause in secondary sequence with optative. Sm. §2196.

109.3. αὐτῷ. The king—i.e., Artaxerxes, not Megabazus.

ἄλλως. "in vain." LSJ s.v. ἄλλως II.3.

111.1. ὅσα μὴ προϊόντες. An elliptical expression to limit the previous statement. If it were filled out, it would be ὅσα κρατεῖν ἐδύναντο μὴ προϊόντες, "as much as they were able to control without advancing . . ."

πολὺ ἐκ τῶν ὅπλων. "far from the space in camp where the arms were stacked." LSJ s.v. ὅπλον II.5.

112.1. Ἑλληνικοῦ πολέμου ἔσχον. "They refrained from war with [other] Greeks." LSJ s.v. ἔχω B.I.3.

112.4. ὑπὲϱ Σαλαμῖνος. "off Salamis." LSJ s.v. ὑπέϱ I.1b. This is the Salamis on the eastern end of Cyprus.

113.1. φευγόντων. "After the battle of Oenophyta, the democratic party in Boeotia had driven out the anti-Athenian oligarchs. But the exiles had recovered some of their lost power" (Marchant, ad loc.—after Classen and Steup). Cf. Arist. *Pol.* 8.2.6.

ἀλλ᾽ ἄττα χωϱία. "some other territory." ἄττα is sometimes used for the indefinite τινά. Sm. §334a. It is not to be confused with ἅττα (with rough breathing), which is an alternative form for the indefinite relative neuter plural ἅτινα. Sm. §339c.

ὡς ἑκάστοις is parallel with ἑαυτῶν χιλίοις ὁπλίταις. The formula ὡς ἕκαστος means "each for himself." Sm. §2997. Hence, "with individual contingents of the allies."

113.3. ἐφ᾽ ᾧ . . . κομιοῦνται. Clause of proviso with future indicative—hence, "on condition that they will get their men back." Sm. §2279.

116.1. αἱ δὲ ἐπὶ Χίου καὶ Λέσβου περιαγγέλλουσαι βοηθεῖν. "The others happened [ἔτυχον] to be carrying around instructions to Chios and Lesbos to come to their aid." Crawley translates, "carrying around orders for reinforcements."

στϱατιώτιδες·. I.e., troop transport ships, rather than ships equipped for naval battles.

116.3. ἐσαγγελθέντων. Neuter plural impersonal participle in the genitive absolute without accompanying noun. Hence, "news having been brought." This construction is used "when a subordinate clause with ὅτι follows upon the participle in the passive"; "The plural [of the participle] is used when the subject of the subordinate clause [here, Φοίνισσαι νῆες] is plural" (Sm. §2072c).

117.1. ἀφάϱκτῳ τῷ στϱατοπέδῳ. This is the camp on shore for the crews of the fleet. It had not been fortified with a stockade. Gomme, ad loc. and pp. 19–20.

118.2. ὄντες μὲν καὶ πϱὸ τοῦ μὴ ταχεῖς ἰέναι ἐς τοὺς πολέμους. μή is anomalous and has not been satisfactorily explained. Perhaps, because it is bracketed by two μή expressions (εἰ μὴ ἐπὶ βραχύ and ἢν μὴ ἀναγκά-ζωνται), it results from a kind of negative momentum. Or perhaps, as Marchant (ad loc.) suggests, μή gives a flavor of generality to the participle (Sm. §2045), as if to say the Spartans are generally the kind of people slow in attacking enemies.

πρὸ τοῦ. "before this time." Here, the article is used as a demonstrative. This happens rarely with prepositions, except with πρό. Sm. §1117.

ἀραμένοις is dative after ἐδόκει and means "by starting, initiating, undertaking." LSJ s.v. ἀείρω IV.4.

118.3. εἰ πολεμοῦσιν ἄμεινον ἔσται. Indirect yes-no question after ἐπηρώτων. Sm. §2671.

ξυλλήψεσθαι, meaning "assist," is here used absolutely (i.e., without a complement). LSJ s.v. συλλαμβάνω VI.1.

119.1. δεηθέντες μὲν καὶ κατὰ πόλεις πρότερον ἑκάστων ἰδίᾳ. "having asked of each of them privately city by city even earlier." In their concern for Potidaea, the Corinthians had, already before the congress at Sparta, sent embassies to the individual cities on their own to ask them to vote for war. ἑκάστων is the genitive of the person after δέομαι. LSJ s.v. δέω II.2.

ὥστε ψηφίσασθαι is not a result expression. ὥστε plus the infinitive is often used with verbs of will and desire instead of the more common simple infinitive. Sm. §2271. So this is equivalent to the simple infinitive after δεηθέντες.

120.1. ὡς οὐ ἐψηφισμένοι τὸν πόλεμόν εἰσι . . . καὶ (οὐ) . . . ξυνήγαγον. "on the grounds that they have not voted for war and that they did not convene us . . ."; i.e., the Corinthians can no longer criticize the Spartans on those grounds, as they did in I.68.2, since they have now done just that. This is a noun clause expressing the substance of the charge that the Corinthians no longer wish to make. It can be regarded as either a causal clause (Sm. §2240) or a simple dependent substantive clause (Sm. §2577).

ἐκ πάντων. "before all others." LSJ s.v. ἐκ I.4.

120.2. φυλάξεσθαι αὐτούς. "to be on guard against them." LSJ s.v. φυλάσσω C.II.1.

τοὺς δὲ μεσόγειαν . . . βουλεύεσθαι. The backbone of this sentence follows.

χρὴ
    τοὺς . . . κατοικουμένους εἰδέναι
            ὅτι . . . ἕξουσι
                ἢν μὴ ἀμύνωσι
    καὶ (τοὺς . . . κατοικουμένους) μὴ κριτὰς τῶν νῦν λεγομένων εἶναι
    δὲ (τοὺς . . . κατοικουμένους) προσδέχεσθαι
                καὶ ἂν προελθεῖν
                    εἰ πρόοιντο
    καὶ (τοὺς . . . κατοικουμένους) βουλεύεσθαι

The contrast is between those living inland (οἱ τὴν μεσόγειαν κατῳ-κημένοι) and those living near the sea (οἱ κατὼ κατῳκημένοι).

χρή takes four infinitives: εἰδέναι, εἶναι, προσδέχεσθαι, and βουλεύ-εσθαι.

κατακομίδην . . . καὶ . . . ἀντίληψιν. "export and exchange [trade]."

ὧν = τούτων ἅ. The relative pronoun, the direct object of δίδωσι, is attracted to the case of its ghost antecedent, which would have been a genitive defining ἀντίληψιν. "A demonstrative pronoun to whose case the relative is attracted, is usually omitted if unemphatic" (Sm. §2522).

ὡς μὴ προσηκόντων. ὡς means "on the grounds that." Sm. §2086. The negative is μὴ because it is influenced by the prohibition "Do not be inept judges." Sm. §2737c.

εἰ . . . πρόοιντο. Third plural aorist optative middle of προίημι. The canonical form would be προεῖντο (< προ⁻έ⁻ι⁻ντο), but this irregular form is confected on the analogy of the thematic optatives. Sm. §§777, 746c. Forms of ⁻μι verbs often drift over into the thematic conjugation. This is the protasis of a potential ("should-would") condition in indirect discourse after προσδέχεσθαι. The apodosis is represented by the infinitive προελθεῖν with ἄν. Usually, προσδέχεσθαι takes a future infinitive, but that would have obscured the indirect form of the potential condition.

A recapitulation of the sentence follows.

It is necessary for those who dwell inland and not on a sea route to understand that unless they come to the defense of those living by the sea [τοῖς κάτω], they will find that the export of their produce and reciprocal exchange of things that the sea grants to the land will be more difficult; and [it is necessary] for them not to be inept critics of the things now said on the grounds that they do not apply [to them]; and [it is necessary for them] to expect someday, if they should abandon the interests of the maritime cities, danger would finally reach them; and [it is necessary for them] to make decisions now affecting themselves no less [than they affect us].

120.3. ἀνδρῶν σωφρόνων. . . . ἀγαθῶν δέ. Predicate genitives, denoting the person whose nature, duty, custom, etc. is to do what is set forth in the infinitive. Sm. §1304. Hence, "It is the custom of wise men to remain quiet . . ."

εὖ δὲ παρασχὸν ἐκ πολέμου πάλιν ξυμβῆναι. παρασχόν is the neuter singular aorist active participle of παρέχω in an accusative absolute. Sm. §2076. Hence, "it being in their power to come to terms again out of a state of war." LSJ s.v. παρέχω A.III.2.

μήτε τῇ κατὰ πόλεμον εὐτυχίᾳ ἐπαίρεσθαι. "not to be elated by their success in war."

μήτε ἡδόμενον ἀδικεῖσθαι. "nor gladly to suffer injustice." The usual explanation for the fact that ἡδόμενον is not plural like the preceding ἀδικουμένους is that it is singular as if τινα had preceded it—i.e., "It is the characteristic of brave men for anyone not to suffer injustice gladly." This explanation has never seemed very convincing to me. I think, rather, that this anacoluthon is introduced in anticipation of the following sentence, where ὁ ὀκνῶν is singular.

120.4. ἀφαιρεθείη. In the active, the verb ἀφαιρέω takes the accusative of the thing and the dative of the person, i.e., "take something (acc.) away from someone (dat.)." In the passive construction here, the dative becomes the subject, and the accusative object, τὸ τερπνόν, remains, i.e., ἀφῃρέθη τι, "he got deprived of something." It is a potential optative here.

τὸ τερπνόν. Neuter adjective for abstract noun (the *schema Thucydideum*).

οὐκ ἐντεθύμηται θράσει ἀπίστῳ ἐπαιρόμενος. The participle ἐπαιρόμενος is in indirect discourse after a verb of perception. Sm. §2110. It is nominative because it refers to the subject of the leading verb. Hence, "He is not in the present enduring state of being aware that he is elated over unfounded self-confidence." LSJ s.v. ἐνθυμέομαι I.1d.

120.5. τυχόντα. With this reading, τυχόντα agrees with πολλὰ γνωσθέντα and takes the genitive ἀβουλοτέρων τῶν ἐναντίων. Further, ἀβουλοτέρων is predicative. Sm. §§1168–69. Hence, "Many things that have been badly planned succeed by finding enemies more unprepared." But some MSS and some editors read τυχόντων, giving a genitive absolute—hence, "Plans succeed when the enemy happens to be more unprepared." For τυγχάνω without a supplementary participle, see Sm. §2119; cf. Thuc. I.32.3.

κατωρθώθη. Empiric aorist. "With adverbs signifying *often, always, sometimes, already, not yet, never*, etc., the aorist expressly denotes a fact of experience" (Sm. §1930). The adjective πολλά is tantamount to such an adverb.

ἐνθυμεῖται γὰρ οὐδεὶς ὁμοῖα τῇ πίστει καὶ ἔργῳ ἐπεξέρχεται. Gomme (ad loc.) says: "'what a man plans in his confident belief in the future is very unlike what he carries out in practice.' This is a satisfactory enough rendering of the MSS reading ὁμοῖα (Forbes, Widmann, Stuart Jones alone of modern editors)." According to this rendering, τῇ πίστει is a dative of means, ὁμοῖα is the direct object of ἐνθυμεῖται, and the particle of comparison is καὶ. Sm. §§1501a, 2875. Hence, literally, "no one plans in confidence things similar to what he accomplishes in fact." But Johann Jacob Reiske (1716–74), one of the heroes of classical scholarship, suggested the reading ὁμοίᾳ here—in his five volumes of *Animadversiones* (1757–66), in which he proposed many corrections in the texts of Greek authors. Gomme continues: "if we read ὁμοίᾳ with Reiske and most others, we translate: 'no one plans and carries out his plan in action with the same confidence.' The essential point is that ὁμοῖα or ὁμοίᾳ τῇ πίστει goes with both verbs."

δοξάζομεν, meaning "imagine, speculate, make plans," is used absolutely.

ἐλλείπομεν. "fall short." LSJ s.v. ἐλλείπω I.3.

121.1. ἀμυνώμεθα. Aorist subjunctive.

αὐτόν. Sc., τὸν πόλεμον.

121.2. κατὰ πολλά. "on many grounds." LSJ s.v. κατά IV.1.

ὁμοίως πάντας ἐς τὰ παραγγελλόμενα ἰόντας. "[because] we will all obey orders together." For the expression ἰέναι ἐς τὰ παραγγελλόμενα, cf. Thuc. III.55.3.

121.4. ἁλίσκονται. Present for future. Hence, "They [the Athenians] will be defeated." LSJ s.v. I.2. "The present is used instead of the future in statements of what is immediate, likely, certain, or threatening" (Sm. §1879).

εἰ δ᾽ ἀντίσχοιεν. Potential conditional clause, emphasizing the possibility, but not the likelihood, of the condition. It is followed by an apodosis in the future (not the optative plus ἄν of a "should-would" condition) and therefore counts as a "mixed condition." Sm. §2361. Hence, "If they should hold out [possible but not likely], we will [certainly] have more time to train our navy."

ὅταν . . . καταστήσωμεν . . . περιεσόμεθα. Here, the eventual temporal clause—ὅταν plus the subjunctive (Sm. §2399)—emphasizes the Corinthians' expectation that they will put their skill on an equal basis with the Athenians when necessary and will consequently prevail.

ὃ . . . προύχουσι. The editors disagree on the interpretation of the syntax here. προέχω, "surpass, excel," is intransitive; therefore, the relative pronoun should be not a direct object but an adverbial accusative, functioning like such words as πολύ, μέγα, and ὅσον. Smyth categorizes these as accusatives of measure and degree. Sm. §1609. This is Marchant's interpretation. But because its antecedent is a missing τοῦτο in the main clause (which is the subject of καθαιρετόν ἐστι) and because it is parallel to the preceding sentences with a neuter relative clause, it should be treated as a true direct object after προέχω. There is a disputed parallel at Soph. Ant. 208, where the MSS read τιμὴν προέξουσ᾽. This is the explanation of Classen and Steup, (ad loc.). The meaning, at any rate, is clear: "Where they excel in skill, that [advantage] can be removed by us through training." It is best, I think, to regard this as a mild anacoluthon driven by the parallelism of the preceding sentence. καθαιρετόν is not the verbal in ⁻τέος, signaling obligation or necessity, but the simple passive verbal adjective in ⁻τος (cognate with the Latin perfect passive participles), signaling possibility. Sm. §§425c, 472. It takes the dative of agent. Sm. §1488.

121.5. ὥστε ἔχειν . . . οἴσομεν. Despite its appearance, ὥστε ἔχειν is not a result phrase. It is an infinitive after a verb of will and desire (Sm. §§1991–92), strengthened with ὥστε, and has the flavor of a purpose clause. Kühner-Gerth 2:8, §473A6. οἴσομεν χρήματα [we will pay money] then has the force of "We will make contributions to have money for this purpose," and the verb οἴσομεν slips over into the category of verbs of will and desire. χρήματα is used twice: as the object of οἴσομεν and as the object of ἔχειν. Cf. Thuc. V.17, ψηφισαμένων ὥστε καταλύεσθαι [having voted to make peace]; IV.132.3; VII.86.3. Cf. also **119.1**.

ἤ is used here in the sense of εἰ δὲ μή, "otherwise." Sm. §2859.

δεινόν ἂν εἴη . . . πάσχειν. Mixed condition with two protases. The apodosis is δεινόν ἂν εἴη, a potential optative—hence, "It would be terrible." The protases are real conditions with future indicatives (οὐκ ἀπεροῦσιν and οὐκ ἄρα δαπανήσομεν) indicating a threat or warning. "The protasis commonly suggests something undesired, or feared" (Sm. §2328). Hence, "It would be terrible if they will not grow weary . . . and [if] we will not pay." δεινόν ἂν εἴη takes an εἰ clause rather than an ὅτι clause because it is tantamount to a verb of emotion. Sm. §2247.

φέροντες οὐκ ἀπεροῦσιν. The lexicons list this verb under ἀπεῖπον because there is no present in fifth-century Attic. Here, it means "fail, grow weary, sink from exhaustion." LSJ s.v. IV.3. It takes a supplementary participle. Sm. §2098. Hence, "they will not grow weary of making contributions."

ἐπὶ δουλείᾳ. "for the purpose of [their own] slavery." LSJ s.v. ἐπί B.III.2.

οὐκ ἀπεροῦσιν and οὐκ ἄρα δαπανήσομεν. Despite the fact that these are protases and should have the negative μή, they have οὐ instead. "When a single εἰ introduces a bimembered protasis *as a whole*, the μέν clause and the δέ clause of that protasis may have οὐ. Such bimembered protases often depend upon a preceding apodosis introduced by αἰσχρόν, ἄτοπον, δεινόν, or θαυμαστόν ἐστι (ἂν εἴη)" (Sm. §2698e).

καὶ ἐπὶ τῷ μὴ ὑπ' ἐκείνων αὐτὰ ἀφαιρεθέντες αὐτοῖς τούτοις κακῶς πάσχειν. The basic construction is the articular infinitive in the dative after the preposition, ἐπὶ τῷ μὴ . . . κακῶς πάσχειν [for the purpose of not suffering ill]. The participle ἀφαιρεθέντες is nominative because it refers to the subject of the "if" clause, ἡμεῖς. In the active, the verb ἀφαιρέω takes the accusative of the thing and the dative of the person, i.e., "take something (acc.) away from someone (dat.)". In the passive construction here, the dative becomes the subject, and the accusative object remains, i.e., ἀφῃρέθη τι, "he got deprived of something." Hence, "for the purpose of not suffering ill by our having been deprived of it [αὐτά—sc., τὰ χρήματα] by them [the Athenians]." αὐτοῖς τούτοις refers again to the money and is a dative of means modifying κακῶς πάσχειν— hence, "to suffer ill by means of this very money."

The upshot follows.

Otherwise, it would be terrible if their allies will not grow weary of paying tribute to support their own slavery, and [it would be terrible] if we also will fail to spend money for the purpose of punishing our enemies and likewise for our own safety, and to avoid suffering harm by means of the very money we have been deprived of at their hands.

At I.120.2, the Corinthians complained that the Athenians deprived the Peloponnesians of money by siphoning off the profits of trade (τὴν κομίδην τῶν ὁραίων). The profits transferred to the Athenians would then be used to finance the Athenian war effort.

122.1. οὖσα. The participle equates ἀπόστασις with παραίρεσις; i.e., the defection of the Athenian allies means the withdrawal of tribute.

ἐπὶ ῥητοῖς. "on set terms, on specified conditions, by definite rules."

ὁ μὲν εὐοργήτως αὐτῷ προσομιλήσας. "the one who meets it [war] with emotions under control."

122.2. ἐνθυμῶμαι. Hortatory subjunctive. Sm. §1797. Hence, "Let us consider that [ὅτι] . . ." LSJ s.v. I.1c.

οἰστὸν ἂν ἦν. "it would be bearable." οἰστός is the verbal adjective of φέρω.

Ἀθηναῖοι ἱκανοί καὶ . . . δυνατώτεροι. This is the main clause, with the copula missing. Sm. §944.

ὥστε εἰ μὴ . . . ἀμυνούμεθα . . . χειρώσονται. Real condition with futures in both protasis and apodosis—a minatory-monitory condition (Sm. §2328) embedded in a result clause.

ἧσσαν. Accusative of the short a-stem feminine noun ἧσσα, "defeat."

φέρουσαν. Participle in indirect discourse agreeing with ἧσσαν after verb of perception.

ἀντικρὺς δουλείαν. "undisguised slavery." The adverb ἀντικρὺς, "openly," serves as an adjective, despite the lack of an article to put it in attributive position (we would expect τὴν ἀντικρὺς δουλείαν). Sm. §1132.

122.3. ὃ καὶ λόγῳ ἐνδοιασθῆναι αἰσχρόν (ἐστι). The antecedent of the neuter relative ὅ is the preceding sentence about slavery, and the infinitive κακοπαθεῖν is parallel to the infinitive ἐνδοιασθῆναι. Hence, "about which [slavery] it is shameful for there to be doubtful discussion, as it is shameful for so many cities to suffer under the rule of one."

ἐν ᾧ. "in which case."

αὐτό. Sc., τὸ ἐλευθεροὶ εἶναι, implied by the preceding sentence.

τύραννον δὲ ἐῶμεν ἐγκαθεστάναι πόλιν. "but we allow a tyrant city to be established [in Greece]." ἐγκαθεστάναι is a perfect active infinitive intransitive (LSJ s.v. ἐγκαθίστημι II), and "in Greece" is easily supplied from the preverb ἐν.

τοὺς δ' ἐν μιᾷ μονάρχους ἀξιοῦμεν καταλύειν. "We think it right to suppress autocrats in any given single [city]."

ὅπως ... ἀπηλλάκται. Indirect question after ἴσμεν. The subject, τάδε, refers to the Corinthians' conduct—namely, failure to establish freedom and allowing a tyrant city to flourish—i.e., to what has just been said. ὅδε usually refers to what is to follow (Sm. §1245) but occasionally refers to what precedes, if it has just been mentioned. Sm. §1247. Cf. Thuc. I.41.1. In the active, the verb ἀπαλλάσσω means "deliver someone (acc.) from something (gen.)." In the middle, it means "be released from something (gen.)." Here the meaning of the perfect middle is "be free from the imputation of" (plus the genitive). LSJ s.v. B.II.6. Hence, "we do not know how this conduct is free from the imputation of the three greatest failings."

οὐ γὰρ πεφευγότες ... μετωνόμασται. The negative οὐ goes with the participle because it states a fact. Sm. §2728. "For you have not in fact avoided them [the failings], and you have moved to that contempt [of an enemy] that destroys most people and that from the fact that it trips up so many, gets its name changed to the opposite meaning, namely, stupidity." Marchant's translation is helpful: "For it is not the case that you are free from these errors in assuming that contempt which has proved ruinous to so many, ... and which from its tendency to trip men up, has received instead (sc. from prudent men) the opposite name of folly."

καταφρόνησις basically means "contempt, disdain for others" but here modulates into the arrogance that underestimates an opponent's strength.

The jingle in the opposition καταφρόνησις/ἀφροσύνη gives something of an apothegmatic flavor to the sentiment.

123.1. τί δεῖ μακρότερον . . . αἰτιᾶσθαι. "What need [is there] to complain further about the past?"

ἐς ὅσον τοῖς νῦν ξυμφέρει. "so far as it helps the present."

περὶ δὲ τῶν ἔπειτα μελλόντων. "concerning the future"—literally, "concerning things that are going to be then."

τοῖς παροῦσι βοηθοῦντας χρὴ ἐπιταλαιπωρεῖν. "It is necessary [for us] to labor yet more concerning the future by preserving present resources." βοηθέω here means "preserve, protect, maintain," and the dative neuter plural participle means "what we have now."

εἰ ἄρα πλούτῳ κτλ. Real condition with present, signaling an admitted fact. Hence, "given the fact that you now excel a little in . . ." Smyth categorizes such clauses as "concessive clauses." Sm. §§2369–82. Usually, clauses that "indicate that the condition which they introduce may be granted without destroying the conclusion" are introduced by εἰ καί (Sm. §2370). Here, εἰ ἄρα is the equivalent. "ἄρα in a conditional protasis denotes that the hypothesis is one of which the possibility has just been realized" (Denniston, *Gr. Part.*², 37). We can translate, "notwithstanding the fact that." προφέρω here means "surpass, excel" (LSJ s.v. IV.2), indicating that the Spartans have surpassed their old situation, when their virtue was the product of labor. Presumably, the Corinthians are referring to the fact—stated by Thucydides in I.19—that the Spartans were now at the height of their power.

κατὰ πολλά goes with θαρσοῦντας. Hence, "with many reasons for boldness." Sm. §1690.2c.

τὰ μὲν φόβῳ, τὰ δὲ ὠφελίᾳ. I.e., on the one hand, some Greeks will join in the struggle out of fear of Athens, whereas, on the other hand, others will do so out of a desire for advantage.

ἠδικημέναις is feminine because of an understood σπονδαῖς.

124.1. ὥστε here simply introduces the main sentence, not a subordinate result clause. Sm. §2255. The main verb is the following imperative μὴ μέλλετε—hence, "so don't delay . . ."

ὑπάρχον. Neuter participle in accusative absolute, parallel with the following genitive absolute. Sm. §2076. The participle is in the accusative absolute because it is impersonal with an infinitive subject. The following genitive absolute is personal.

εἴπερ βεβαιότατον τὸ ταὐτὰ ξυμφέροντα καὶ πόλεσι καὶ ἰδιώταις εἶναι. Real condition with present indicative (the missing copula ἐστί) indicating an admitted fact. "Given the fact that it is most secure for there to be the same interests for both cities and individuals [i.e., for cities and individuals to have the same interests]." Smyth treats this construction rather too briefly under "Causal Clauses." Sm. §2246. Cf. Thuc. I.77.6. The apodosis of this real condition is the negative imperative μὴ μέλλετε.

οὗ πρότερον ἦν τοὐναντίον. "the opposite of which was formerly true." In earlier conflicts, the Dorians usually had the upper hand.

ὡς οὐκέτι ἐνδέχεται κτλ. The rest of the sentence is dependent on ἐνδέχεται, the verb of this causal clause, which means "since it is no longer possible" (LSJ s.v. II.2) and is followed by two infinitive phrases as subjects.

> (ἡμᾶς) περιμένοντας
> τοὺς μὲν βλάπτεσθαι
> τοὺς δὲ μὴ πάσχειν.

Hence, since "it is no longer possible, if we [all] wait around, for some of us [i.e., "us Corinthians"] to be already harmed and for others [sc., "you Spartans"] not to suffer the same soon after." The negative μή with the infinitive πάσχειν presents a problem. Usually, after a negative leading verb, a negative infinitive will have μὴ οὐ. Thus, we would expect οὐκέτι ἐνδέχεται μὴ οὐ πάσχειν. Sm. §§2745–46. Occasionally, it may have simple μή. Sm. §2749. But then the πολὺ ὕστερον needs a negative too. The sentence means "since it is no longer possible to avoid suffering the same thing, and that not much later." By a kind of anacoluthon, we must assume that the μή serves both the infinitive and the adverbial phrase. Alternatively, if we had μὴ οὐ οὐ πολὺ ὕστερον, the two οὐ's would cancel each other out. In any case, it seems that Thucydides is trying to avoid a train wreck of accumulated negatives here.

The second infinitive phrase has an embedded conditional clause, a real condition with future protasis, signaling something unpleasant or regrettable. Sm. §2328. Its verb, γνωσόμεθα, is a verb of perception taking a participle in indirect discourse, which is nominative because it refers to the subject of the leading verb. Sm. §2106. Hence, "if it comes to be known that we have met together, on the one hand, but that we do not dare to defend ourselves, on the other hand."

124.2. ἀπ' αὐτοῦ. Understand πολέμου.

διὰ πλείονος. "lasting a long time." This temporal construction in attributive position modifies τῆς . . . εἰρήνης peace.

ἀφ' ἡσυχίας δὲ μὴ πολεμῆσαι οὐχ ὁμοίως ἀκίνδυνον. "But failure to shift to war out of a desire to avoid trouble is, by the same token, not without risk." ἀφ' ἡσυχίας is not easy to translate. It is contrasted with ἐκ πολέμου [by reason of war], and Classen and Steup (ad loc.) suggest that ἀπό means the same as ἐκ by Thucydides' frequent habit of variation with prepositions. But there also seems to be some flavor of reluctance to shift from inactivity to action. ὁμοίως does not really mark a direct parallelism, because Thucydides reverses field. He has the Corinthians say, "Keep your eye on eventual peace [strengthened by war], but do not let that prevent you from entering upon this necessary war. Inaction to avoid trouble is as risky [ὁμοίως] as going to war."

124.3. παραστησώμεθα ἐπελθόντες. The object of both the finite verb and the participle is πόλιν. παρίστημι here means "bring to terms, subject to force." LSJ s.v. C.II.1. παραστησώμεθα is the sigmatic transitive aorist subjunctive.

125.2. δεδογμένον αὐτοῖς. Accusative absolute. Sm. §2076B. Hence, "the decision having been made by them." As the postpositive μέν indicates, εὐθύς goes with the next constituent, i.e., ἀδύνατα ἦν.

ἀδύνατα ἦν ἐπιχειρεῖν. Thucydides often uses the neuter plural adjective (here, ἀδύνατα) instead of the singular in impersonal constructions, i.e., those where an infinitive is the grammatical subject. Sm. §1052. Cf. **7.1.**

καθισταμένοις ὧν ἔδει. "to them putting in order what was necessary." καθισταμένοις is a dative of possession. Hence, "Their delay was . . ." The present middle of καθίστημι can be transitive. LSJ s.v. A.II.2b.

ἐνιαυτὸς μὲν οὐ διατριβή. Two nouns in a copulative sentence: "The delay [LSJ s.v. διατριβή II] was not a year." ἔλασσον is neuter, rather than feminine to agree with διατριβή, because it is in fact an adverb, "more quickly [they prepared]." LSJ s.v. ἐλάσσων V. Cf. Thuc. IV.67.2; Hdt. 7.39.2. Hence, "Their delay was not a year—indeed, [they prepared] more quickly." This has caused some puzzlement, and Gomme (ad loc.) asks, "Is Thucydides stressing the delay or the comparative rapidity?" Gomme believes he is stressing the delay: "in spite of their resolution that there was to be no delay, nearly a year passed before the invasion."

126.1. ὅπως . . . εἴη . . . ἢν μή τι ἐσακούωσιν. Eventual condition embedded in a purpose clause. The original form would be ἢν μή τι ἐσακούωσιν, πρόφασις ἔσται, (in Smyth's terms, a future more vivid), "If ever they fail to heed, there will be a pretext." When this is embedded in a purpose clause in secondary sequence, the main verb, the future, becomes present optative (Sm. §2196; it would become future optative only in indirect discourse or after verbs of effort [Sm. §1862b]), and the subordinate "if" clause may remain unchanged. Sm. §2610 (this section refers to indirect discourse, but the principle applies here).

126.5. ἑαυτῷ τι προσήκειν Ὀλύμπια νενικηκότι. "that the festival of Olympian Zeus was somehow appropriate to him because he was an Olympic victor." Joined with verbs, the neuter unaccented τι means "somewhat, any degree at all." LSJ s.v. τις A.II.11c.

126.6. εἰ δέ . . . "but whether . . ." This is not a condition but an indirect yes-no question after κατενόησε and ἐδήλου.

θύουσι πολλὰ οὐχ ἱερεῖα, ἀλλ᾿ ⟨ἁγνὰ⟩ θύματα ἐπιχώρια. "They sacrifice many offerings, not animal victims, but bloodless cakes peculiar to the country." The lexicographer Pollux, of the second century A.D., says (1.26), "Thucydides calls them ἁγνὰ θύματα in contrast with τὰ αἱμάσσοντα καὶ σφαττόμενα," that is, "holy (bloodless) cakes in contrast with bloody slaughtered victims." On the evidence of Pollux, editors supply ἁγνὰ and interpret it to mean "bloodless." The scholiast to Thucydides says, "θύματα ἐπιχώρια, τινὰ πέμματα εἰς ζώων μορφὰς τετυπωμένα [cakes shaped into the forms of animals]. Editors have accepted the conjecture πολλὰ of C. F. Hermann, instead of the πολλοί of the MSS, because "many people" would not be consistent with πανδημεί [with the whole people]. Carl (or Karl) Friedrich Hermann (1804–55), professor at Marburg and Göttingen, is to be distinguished from the far greater Gottfried Hermann (1772–1848), professor at Leipzig.

126.8. αὐτοκράτορσι modifies τοῖς ἐννέα ἄρχουσι. Thus, the nine archons had a free hand to do whatever they chose.

φλαυρῶς εἶχον. "were in bad shape." This is a common idiom, ἔχω plus an adverb being equivalent to εἰμί plus a predicate adjective. Sm. §1438.

καί τινες καί. The first καί is connective, the second καί an adverb intensifying ἀπέθνῃσκον. Sm. §2881. Hence, "and some even were dying."

126.11. ἐφ᾽ ᾧ μηδὲν κακὸν ποιήσουσιν. This clause is dependent on ἀναστήσαντες. ἐφ᾽ ᾧ introduces a clause of proviso (Sm. §2279) and means "on the condition that." It takes future indicative (cf. Thuc. I.103.1). The negative of a clause of proviso is μή. Hence, "[The archons] raised them up [from their suppliant position] with the promise [proviso] that they [the archons] would do them no harm."

ἐπιτετραμμένοι τὴν φυλάκην. "those entrusted with guarding [them]." ἐπιτρέπω takes an accusative of the thing entrusted and a dative of the person to whom it is entrusted. The middle transformation makes the original dative the subject and leaves the accusative as it was.

127.1. τοῦτο δὴ τὸ ἄγος κτλ. The particle δή resumes the argument after a long digression. Sm. §2846. Denniston, Gr. Part.², 225 (13).

δῆθεν. "Expressing, not incredulity, but contempt or indignation: 'forsooth'" (Denniston, Gr. Part.², 265 f.); "commonly used of apparent or pretended truth, and mostly with an ironical tone" (Sm. §2849). The force of the particle makes it clear that the Spartans are only hypocritically pretending to be concerned for the honor of the gods. Their real motive is exposed in the next participial phrases.

προσεχόμενον αὐτῷ. αὐτῷ refers to ἄγος.

τὰ ἀπὸ τῶν Ἀθηναίων. "what they wanted from the Athenians."

127.2. παθεῖν ἄν ... οἴσειν. The switch to the future from potential optative (represented by the infinitive plus ἄν in indirect discourse) marks the difference between the remote possibility, which is not expected, and the future certainty, which is expected.

τὸ μέρος. Neuter accusative used as an adverb—hence, "partly." Sm. §§1606, 1609.

128.2. Χαλκιοίκου refers to a temple and statue of Athena on the Spartan citadel, which were made of bronze. Pausanias (the second-century A.D. author of a guidebook to Greece—not to be confused with the Spartan regent who is the subject of this story) says (3.17.2), τόν τε ναὸν ὁμοίως καὶ τὸ ἄγαλμα ἐποιήσαντο Ἀθηνᾶς χαλκοῦν.

128.3. Ἑρμιονίδα. "from the town of Hermione"—in Argolis at the southern tip of the peninsula called Acte.

πράσσειν. Infinitive of purpose after a verb of motion (ἀφικνεῖται). Kühner-Gerth 2:16–17, §472A7. Sm. §2009. This construction is rare in prose, where the future participle is more usual. Sm. §2065.

128.4. ἀπὸ τοῦδε. I.e., from what is to follow in the next sentence, introduced by γάρ.

128.5. αὐτό refers to Byzantium.

ἑάλωσαν. Third plural aorist active indicative of ἁλίσκομαι, "fall into an enemy's hands, be captured." The citation form is ἑάλων, conjugated like ἔγνων. Sm. §682.

128.6. Ἐρετριῶς. Genitive singular of Ἐρετριεύς. The noun is declined like βασιλεύς (Sm. §275), but in the genitive, the expected ⁻ιέως contracts to ⁻ιῶς. For this process, see Schwyzer, 252.

129.1. ἀπαλλάξαντα. "having replaced."

ἐπιστολὴν ἀντεπιτίθει αὐτῷ is a pregnant construction, or brachylogy. Sm. §3017. Hence, "Xerxes in response gave a letter to Artabazus [αὐτῷ] [with orders] to send it on [διαπέμψαι] to Pausanias [παρὰ Παυσανίαν]."

129.3. μὴ ἐπισχέτω ὥστε ἀνεῖναι πράσσειν. Although ἐπισχέτω might at first seem to be a verb of hindering, it does not take the construction of a verb of hindering, which would be a simple infinitive without ὥστε. Sm. §2038. Thus, ὥστε ἀνεῖναι is an ordinary result expression. ἀνεῖναι is the aorist infinitive of ἀνίημι, "neglect." LSJ s.v. II.7b. Hence, "let neither day nor night hold you back, with the result [if they did] that you [would] neglect to accomplish any of the promises you made to me." For ἀνίημι with the infinitive, cf. the near parallel μεθιᾶσι τὰ δέοντα πράττειν at Xen. Mem. 2.1.33.

κεκωλύσθω. Perfect middle imperative. The verb is used absolutely. Hence, "Let there be no hindrance due to . . ." Some would argue that the subject of κεκωλύσθω is an unexpressed ταῦτα—hence, "Let these things not be hindered." It may be that the subject of κεκωλύσθω is the relative clause ὧν ἐμοὶ ὑπισχνῇ.

130.1. ἦρτο. Third singular middle indicative pluperfect of ἀείρω, "lift." Hence, "he was in a continuous state of being lifted up"; i.e., he became puffed up with self-regard. This precise usage is omitted from LSJ (although it may be implied by entry II). Cf. LSJ s.v. ἐπαίρω II.2 ("to be elated").

130.2. δυσπρόσοδον. "unapproachable, isolated from others."

μετέστη. Third singular intransitive root aorist meaning "changed its allegiance"—to the Athenians. LSJ s.v. μεθίστημι B.I.4.

131.1. πράσσων τε ἐσηγγέλλετο αὐτοῖς. Personal construction. Hence, "He was reported to them [the Spartans] to be scheming with the barbarians." For the idiom πράσσειν ἔς τινα, cf. LSJ s.v. πράσσω I.6. Some MSS read πρὸς τοὺς βαρβάρους.

εἶπον τοῦ κήρυκος μὴ λείπεσθαι. "They ordered [him] not to lag behind the herald." LSJ s.v. λείπω B.II.2. This means he should accompany the herald back to Sparta.

εἰ δὲ μή. "otherwise." Sm. §2346d.

πόλεμον αὐτῷ Σπαρτιάτας προαγορεύειν. Indirect discourse dependent on εἶπον. Hence, "[They said] that the Spartiates declare war on him."

131.2. διαπραξάμενος. "by intrigue." LSJ s.v. IV.

132.1. ἄν . . . ἐτιμωροῦντο. Potential imperfect. Sm. §1784. Hence, "[by trusting to which] they could have punished [such a man]." βεβαίως goes with πιστεύοντες.

132.2. ὑποψίας . . . μὴ ἴσος βούλεσθαι εἶναι τοῖς παροῦσι. "reasons for suspicion, namely, to be unwilling to be equal to the current [ways of doing things]." Warner translates, "unwilling to abide by normal standards." The suspicion is defined by the infinitive phrase, which has a nominative predicate adjective because it refers to the subject of the main verb (παρεῖχε). Sm. §1973. The infinitive phrase (not in indirect discourse, for then the negative would have been οὐ) is in apposition to the noun ὑποψίας. Sm. §1987.

εἴ τί που ἐξεδεδιῄτητο τῶν καθεστώτων νομίμων. "whether he had in any way at all departed from the customary mode of life." ἐξεδεδιῄτητο is the pluperfect middle of ἐκδιαιτάω, a denominative alpha-contract verb based on the noun δίαιτα, "way of living, mode of life." ἐκδιαιτάω means to "change one's habits from something (gen.)." The clause is an indirect question after ἀνεσκόπουν.

καὶ ὅτι . . . ἠξίωσεν κτλ. This noun clause also follows on ἀνεσκόπουν. Hence, "They were examining to see whether . . . and [they were examining] the fact that he had presumed . . ."

132.3. ἐδόκει. The subject of ἐδόκει is the preceding action, i.e., ἐπιγρά-ψασθαι. ἀδίκημα is a predicate noun.

ἐπεί γε δὴ ἐν τούτῳ καθειστήκει. Denniston (Gr. Part.², 245) calls the combination ἐπεί γε δή "emphatic limitative." By "limitative," he means the "predominating use of γε" (Gr. Part.², 140), i.e., "at least." Hence, "at least when he indeed got himself into this situation." The pluperfect of καθίστημι, "come into a certain state, be" (LSJ s.v. B.V), has simple imperfect meaning.

παρόμοιον . . . τῇ παρούσῃ διανοίᾳ. "in accordance with his present scheme." Thus, the offense of setting up the inscription is very similar to the arrogance of his scheming with the Persians.

A recapitulation of the sentence follows.

> However, [the action] of Pausanias seemed even then [i.e., when he set up the inscription] a crime, and once he got himself into this trouble [Medism] at any rate, it [the inscription] appeared much more to have been done [then] in accord with his present attitude [of Medism].

132.5. ἠξίωσαν. The subject is the Spartans.

μὴ ταχεῖς εἶναι. The infinitive is in apposition to the noun τρόπῳ. Sm. §1987. βουλεῦσαι is an epexegetical infinitive, functioning like an accusative of respect, qualifying the adjective ταχεῖς. Sm. §2001.

πρίν γε δὴ . . . γίγνεται. "at least until, indeed." After a negative clause, πρίν means "until." When it takes the indicative, a definite time is expressed. Sm. §2432. Hence, "until [the messenger] in fact and indeed actually became an informant."

κατὰ ἐνθύμησίν τινα ὅτι. Literally, "in accordance with some notice that . . ." LSJ s.v. κατά B.IV. Thucydides might have said simply ἐνθυμηθείς, "having noticed," but this way he avoids the clash of participles with δείσας.

ἵνα, ἢν ψευσθῇ τῆς δόξης ἢ καὶ ἐκεῖνός τι μεταγράψαι αἰτήσῃ, μὴ ἐπιγνῷ. The outermost clause here is the negative purpose clause ἵνα . . . μὴ ἐπιγνῷ [so he [Pausanias] might not find out]. Embedded in the purpose clause are two protases connected by the coordinating conjunction ἤ. ἢν ψευσθῇ τῆς δόξης means "if he [Argilos] ever be mistaken in his opinion." It is an eventual condition. Cf. LSJ s.v. ψεύδω A.I.3 (passive with gen.). The second protasis, ἢν . . . ἐκεῖνός τι μεταγράψαι αἰτήσῃ, means "if ever he [Pausanias] asked for it back to change something." Notice that this narration is in the historical present tense. Sm. §1883.

αὐτὸν ηὗρεν ἐγγεγραμμένον κτείνειν. "He found it written to kill him." The infinitive phrase αὐτὸν κτείνειν is the object of the verb, and the perfect middle participle ἐγγεγραμμένον is predicative. The infinitive phrase can also be understood as an indirect imperative, corresponding to an active construction, Παυσανίαν ἐγγεγραφότα αὐτὸν κτείνειν— hence, "[he found that] Pausanias had written that [they] kill him." Presumably, what stood in the letter was a direct imperative, κτείνετε τοῦτον.

133.1. ἀπὸ παρασκευῆς. "by arrangement."

σκηνησαμένου διπλῆν διαφράγματι καλύβην. "having taken up quarters in a hut double by virtue of a partition."

ὡς αὐτόν. Here, ὡς is an "improper" preposition, i.e., a preposition that is not used as a preverb. ὡς plus the accusative is used "of persons only, . . . after verbs expressing or implying motion" (Sm. §1702). Hence, "[Pausanias having come] to him."

τά τε περὶ αὐτοῦ. This is a misprint in the OCT. It should read αὑτοῦ, with a rough breathing (otherwise, it would refer to Pausanias).

ὡς... παραβάλοιτο. In the middle, παραβάλλω is a gambling term meaning "throw one's money on the table" and, hence, "put at risk, endanger." Gomme, ad loc. LSJ (s.v. A.II.1b) cites only one late instance of the gambling term. But cf. Thuc. II.44.3, III.14.1, III.65.3, V.113. παραβάλοιτο and the ironic προτιμηθείη are optatives in indirect discourse in secondary sequence after the leading verb ᾔσθοντο, through the participle ἀποφαίνοντος, which governs the ὡς clauses.

(ὡς) προτιμηθείη δέ. Ironic. By its position after παραβάλοιτο, this phrase marks the contrast between his service and his reward. Hence, "that he was rewarded by being chosen..." προτιμάω means "to be honored before others, to be selected." LSJ s.v. I.2. ἀποθανεῖν is thus an infinitive of purpose after a verb of choosing. Sm. §2009.

οὐκ ἐῶντος ὀργίζεσθαι. οὐκ ἐάω (with οὐ adherescent) means "forbid." Sm. §2692a. Hence, "told him not to be angry."

ἀνάστασις. "safe removal from the temple."

ἀξιοῦντος. "begging him."

τὰ πρασσόμενα. Sc., πρὸς βασιλέα. Hence, "the business with the king."

134.1. λέγεται... προκαταφυγεῖν. The backbone of this sentence is λέγεται (impersonal) αὐτὸν γνῶναι... χωρῆσαι... καὶ προκαταφυγεῖν [The story goes that he recognized... and ran... and escaped]. αὐτὸν μέλλοντα is the accusative subject of γνῶναι. The ὡς εἶδε clause ("as he saw") is dependent on the infinitive of indirect discourse, γνῶναι. λέγεται can take either a personal construction (Sm. §1982) or, as here, an impersonal construction (Sm. §2017b).

ἑνὸς μὲν τῶν ἐφόρων τὸ πρόσωπον προσιόντος ὡς εἶδε. "as he saw the face of one of the ephors who was approaching."

εὐνοίᾳ. "out of goodwill [toward Pausanias]."

134.2. ὑστέρησαν τῇ διώξει. "They were too late in their pursuit."

τὰς θύρας... ἀπῳκοδόμησαν. "They walled up the doors."

ἀπολαβόντες. Here ἀπολαμβάνω has the meaning "lock in." LSJ s.v. IV.

134.3. ὥσπερ εἶχεν. "just as he was."

134.4. ὡς ἄγος . . . ὄν. Accusative absolute. Sm. §§2076, 2078. Thucydides uses ὡς with the accusative absolute many times (e.g., I.28.1). Here, it marks that this is the judgment of the goddess. Sm. §2086d.

ὡς ἀντὶ Παυσανίου. Literally, "as instead of Pausanias," i.e., "as a substitute for Pausanias."

135.1. ὡς . . . κρίναντος. Genitive absolute with ὡς indicating the opinion or pretense of the Athenians. Sm. §2086d.

135.2. ξυνεπῃτιῶντο. συνεπαιτιάομαι, "accuse also in addition," takes the accusative of the person and the genitive of the charge. Sm. §1375.

135.3. οἷς εἴρητο ἄγειν ὅπου ἂν περιτύχωσιν. "to whom it had been commanded to [take him] and bring [him to Athens] wherever they encountered [him]." The omission of an explicit object (brachylogy) is frequent when it can easily be supplied from the context. Sm. §3018k. ἄγειν, the pregnant construction, supposes λαβεῖν καὶ ἄγειν. Sm. §3044.

136.2. κατὰ πύστιν ᾗ χωροίη. "in accordance with inquiry where he went." ᾗ χωροίη is an indirect question in secondary sequence (Sm. §2677) after the noun πύστιν. It is in secondary sequence because the formally present tenses of the main verbs are semantically historical. Sm. §§1883, 1858.

καταλῦσαι. καταλύω παρά τινα means "seek hospitality from someone, go and lodge with someone." LSJ s.v. II.2.

136.4. οὐκ ἀξιοῖ . . . φεύγοντα τιμωρεῖσθαι. ἀξιόω (with οὐ adherescent) means "he [Themistocles] regards it as unworthy." Sm. §§2691, 2692a. Some prefer to translate, "begged him not to." In the middle, τιμωρέω means "take vengeance on someone (acc.)." LSJ s.v. I.3.

εἴ τι ἄρα αὐτὸς ἀντεῖπεν αὐτῷ ᾿Αθηναίων δεομένῳ. Real condition in the past tense, signaling an actuality. Hence, "given the fact, after all, that he himself [Themistocles] had denied him [Admetus] something when he [Admetus] made a request of the Athenians." ἄρα marks the protasis as something only just realized ("if after all"). Denniston, Gr. Part.², 37f. The scholiast reports that Admetus had asked for an alliance with the Athenians and that Themistocles was instrumental in turning him down.

καὶ γὰρ ἂν ὑπ' ἐκείνου πολλῷ ἀσθενεστέρου ἐν τῷ παρόντι κακῶς πάσχειν is indirect discourse, even though there is no explicit verb of saying. Sm. §2630. It is a potential optative in indirect discourse with ἄν and the infinitive. Sm. §1845. ἐκείνου is a genitive of comparison after ἀσθενεστέρου, the object of ὑπό. The meaning as the OCT has it is "he [Themistocles] might be the victim of one far weaker than he [Admetus]"; i.e., Themistocles was at anyone's mercy (Gomme, ad loc.). Some editors (Stahl and Hude) conjecture ἀσθενέστερος, which would give the meaning "he [Themistocles], being weaker [than Admetus], would be treated badly by him [Admetus]"; i.e., Admetus would be treating a weaker man badly. This then leads logically to the next sentiment, that it is ignoble to take vengeance on those weaker than you are.

αὐτός = Themistocles; ἐκείνῳ = Admetus.

χρείας τινός . . . καὶ οὐκ ἐς τὸ σῶμα σῴζεσθαι ἐναντιωθῆναι. ἐναντιόομαι is a passive deponent in the aorist and takes a dative of the person opposed (ἐκείνῳ) and a genitive of the matter opposed (χρείας τινός). The construction with ἐναντιωθῆναι changes from a genitive to the logically parallel prepositional phrase plus the articular infinitive. With the accusative, ἐς means "in regard to." LSJ s.v. IV.2. Hence, "that he [Themistocles] opposed him [Admetus] in regard to some request of his [Admetus], but not in regard to saving his life [body]."

εἰπὼν ὑφ' ὧν καὶ ἐφ' ᾧ διώκεται is parenthetical and not part of the indirect discourse. εἰπὼν is nominative because it agrees with the subject of the preceding δηλοῖ (i.e., Themistocles).

σωτηρίας ἂν τῆς ψυχῆς. The ἄν after ἐκεῖνον δέ, which marks the infinitive (ἀποστερῆσαι) representing a potential optative, is repeated after the parenthesis. σωτηρίας τῆς ψυχῆς [saving of his life] is synonymous with τὸ σῶμα σῴζεσθαι. It is genitive after ἀποστερέω, which should take both a genitive of the object and an accusative of the person; but by brachylogy (Sm. §3018k), the accusative is omitted, since it is clear from the object in the protasis, εἰ ἐκδοίη αὐτόν. LSJ s.v. ἀποστερέω; Sm. §1630.

137.1. ὁ δέ. The δέ changes the subject to Admetus.

βουλόμενον. I.e., Themistocles, since he wanted to make his way to the king. This is a causal participle. Sm. §2064.

τὴν ἑτέραν θάλασσαν. I.e., the Aegean. The Molossi lived near the Adriatic coast, around Dodona.

137.2. εἰ μὴ σώσει . . . ἐρεῖν. Real condition with futures in both halves—i.e., a minatory-monitory condition in indirect discourse, embodying a threat, which is embedded in indirect discourse after ἔφη. Sm. §2328.

τὴν δὲ ἀσφαλείαν . . . γένηται. The whole sentence is in implied indirect discourse. ἀσφαλείαν is the subject of the copulative infinitive εἶναι, and the infinitive phrase μηδὲν ἐκβῆναι serves as the predicate noun. Hence, "[He said] that [his] safety consisted in no one disembarking from the ship until such time as the voyage is resumed."

πειθομένῳ. Conditional participle. Hence, "if he obeyed." Sm. §2067.

ἀποσαλεύσας. "lying at anchor in the roadstead." The simple verb σαλεύω means "to be tossed about"—hence, "ride at anchor."

ὑπὲρ τοῦ στατοπέδου. "some distance from the Athenian squadron." When used of ships, ὑπέρ means "off a place." LSJ s.v. A.I.1b. στατόπεδον here means a naval squadron. LSJ s.v. II.

137.3. ἐθεράπευσε. "conciliated." LSJ s.v. II.2.

κάτω . . . ἄνω. In the context of dry land, κάτω means "toward the coast," and ἄνω means "inland." Hence, "one of the coastal Persians."

137.4. ὅτι may introduce direct discourse and function like quotation marks. Sm. §2590a.

ὅσον . . . ἀμυνόμην. "for so long as I defended myself out of necessity against your father when he attacked me."

ἐμοί . . . ἐκείνῳ. Datives of advantage and disadvantage after ἐγένετο. Sm. §1481. Hence, "the retreat happened safely for me and dangerously for him." LSJ s.v. γίγνομαι I.3. ἐν τῷ ἀσφάλει and ἐν ἐπικινδύνῳ are adverbial phrases.

πάλιν goes with ἀποκομιδή. Hence, "the retreat back [to Persia]."

γράψας . . . διάλυσιν. This parenthesis is a comment of Thucydides and does not form part of the letter. The participle is loosely connected to ἐδήλου ἡ γραφή by a slight anacoluthon. Cf. Thuc. I.87.2.

138.2. αὐτῷ. I.e., Artaxerxes.

προϋπάρχουσαν ἀξίωσιν. "his previously existing reputation."

ἀπὸ τοῦ πεῖραν διδοὺς ξυνετὸς φαίνεσθαι. "from the fact that he appeared intelligent and capable as he [regularly] gave proof." He gave proof constantly of his capacity, and from the resulting appearance of intelligence, he became great among the Persians. διδοὺς and ξυνετὸς are nominative because they refer to the omitted subject of the infinitive, which is the same as the subject of the main verb, γίγνεται. Sm. §1973.

138.3. διαφερόντως τι. "rather preeminently, rather specially." The indefinite τι with adverbs (e.g., ἄγαν τι, πάνυ τι) "may strengthen or weaken an assertion, apologize for a comparison, and in general qualify a statement" (Sm. §1268). Stahl argued that the expression went with the μᾶλλον ἑτέρου—hence, "rather markedly more than anyone else." Others take it with θαυμάσαι.

ἐς αὐτό refers to the preceding, namely, his appearing to be intelligent.

θαυμάσαι. An epexegetical infinitive (accusative of respect) with the adjective ἄξιος, specifying in what respect the adjective is true. Greek uses an active infinitive where English expects a passive. Hence, "worthy with respect to admiring" (the English parallel would be "worthy of being admired"). Sm. §§1712, 2006.

ἐς αὐτήν. "with respect to it [ξύνεσιν]." Hence, "without advance study to benefit his native understanding, nor with subsequent second thoughts." Marchant (ad loc.) explains it thus: "his opinion was not based on previous knowledge, nor, after giving it, had he to modify it because he found he was wrong." Some argue that these participles refer specifically to the time before he entered politics (προμαθών) and to the time once he had entered politics (ἐπιμαθών)—hence, "without previous education before he entered politics and without having to take advice from others once he had entered politics."

γνώμων γνώμονος. "a judge, interpreter."

εἰκαστής. "a guesser, diviner."

κρῖναι ἱκανῶς οὐκ ἀπήλλακτο. "he was not removed from judging competently." In this litotes, ἀπήλλακτο is the pluperfect middle of ἀπαλλάσω, signifying a continuous state in the past. Sm. §1952. LSJ s.v. B.II.6. Lattimore translates, "he was not incapacitated from judging accurately."

αὐτοσχεδιάζειν. "speak offhand, extemporaneously, improvise."

138.6. ὡς ἐπὶ προδοσίᾳ φεύγοντος. "on the grounds that he was exiled on a charge of treason." φεύγοντος is a genitive of possession with ὀστᾶ, and the participle is introduced by ὡς to indicate that this is the ground of belief of the Athenians. Sm. §2086. Cf. LSJ s.v. ἐπί B.III.1.

139.1. προύλεγον . . . καθελοῦσι μὴ ἂν γίγνεσθαι πόλεμον. μὴ ἂν γίγνεσθαι is a potential optative in indirect discourse. καθελοῦσι, a conditional participle, refers to the Athenians and is a dative with γίγνεσθαι, meaning "to happen to someone." καθαιρέω here means "repeal, rescind." LSJ s.v. II.4. In direct discourse, this would have been a potential condition: εἰ καθέλοιτε, οὐκ ἂν γένοιτο ὑμῖν πόλεμος. The usual explanation for the fact that the negative of the infinitive is here μή (instead of the expected οὐ) is that προύλεγον has the flavor of a command: the indirect command would be προύλεγον μὴ γίγνεσθαι. The two meanings, potential and imperative, seem to have become mixed. Cf. Thuc. I.140.4, V.49.5, VI.102.4; Goodwin, *Moods and Tenses*, §685.

139.2. ἐπικαλοῦντες. ἐπικαλέω means "bring an accusation of some transgression (acc.) against someone (dat.)." LSJ s.v. IV.1.

ἐπεργασίαν. "encroachment." "The 'sacred land' was on the borders of the Megarid and Attica and sacred to the Goddesses of Eleusis. The 'undefined land,' not further specified here, was apparently some strip between the two territories which it had been agreed to leave neutral" (Gomme, ad loc.)

139.3. ἀφεῖτε. Second plural root aorist optative of ἀφίημι.

γνώμας σφίσιν αὐτοῖς προυτίθεσαν. Literally, "they proposed opinions to themselves." LSJ s.v. προτίθημι II.4. προτιθέναι γνώμας became a technical term meaning "hold a debate." Cf. Thuc. III.36.5.

139.4. ἐπ᾽ ἀμφότερα [on both sides] is explained by the three ὡς χρή clauses meaning "to go to war or not to let the Megarian Decree be an impediment to peace but to rescind it." The χρή is omitted in the second and third clauses by brachylogy. Sm. §3017.

140.1. τῆς μὲν γνώμης . . . ἔχομαι. In the middle and with the genitive, ἔχω means "cling to, hold to." LSJ s.v. C.I.2.

τὰς γνώμας τρεπομένους. Participle in indirect discourse after a verb of knowing. Sm. §2106. Strictly, "being changed with respect to their opinions"—hence, "change their opinion."

δικαιόω. "call on, urge, demand as a right." This verb, somewhat stronger than the usual ἀξιόω, takes an infinitive of will and desire (which is really an indirect imperative)—here, βοηθεῖν. Sm. §1992a. Hence, "I call on those of you who are persuaded to support the common decisions." The direct form would be βοηθεῖτε.

ἢν ἄρα τι καὶ σφαλλώμεθα. Eventual condition embedded within the δικαιῶ clause. ἄρα τι marks what is undesirable. Sm. §2796. καί means "even." Hence, "Even if in some way [which I hope will not happen] we fail."

μηδὲ κατορθοῦντας τῆς ξυνέσεως μεταποιεῖσθαι is parallel to βοηθεῖν after δικαιῶ and means "or otherwise not to claim some share of the credit for wisdom if we succeed." LSJ s.v. μεταποιέω II (middle with genitive). Logically, κατορθοῦντας is parallel with the ἢν σφαλλώμεθα clause; but grammatically, there is an anacoluthon. It cannot be the accusative subject of μεταποιεῖσθαι, which is implied from the ἀναπειθομένους. Classen and Steup (ad loc.) say there is an unmarked change of subject. Perhaps it can be regarded as an accusative absolute. Sm. §2078a.

A recapitulation of the sentence follows.

> And I call on those of you who are persuaded [by me] to support the decisions made in common, even if [god forbid] we fail, or otherwise [I call on you] not to claim a share of the credit for intelligence when we succeed.

ἐνδέχεται. "it is possible" (impersonal). Hence, "for it is possible for the contingency of events to proceed no less irrationally than even human plans."

140.2. εἰρημένον. I.e., stipulated in the Thirty Years' Truce.

δίκας . . . διδόναι καὶ δέχεσθαι. "to make an offer of arbitration and to accept an offer of arbitration."

ἐπιτάσσοντες ἤδη καὶ οὐκέτι αἰτιώμενοι. "giving orders now [like superiors] and no longer making requests [like equals]." The temporal expressions ἤδη and οὐκέτι mark a change in the Spartan attitude. Crawley translates, "dropping the tone of expostulation and adopting that of command."

140.4. ἂν πολεμεῖν . . . εἰ . . . μὴ καθέλοιμεν. Potential condition in indirect discourse after νομίζω.

ὅπερ μάλιστα προύχονται, εἰ καθαιρεθείη, μὴ ἂν γίγνεσθαι τὸν πόλε-μον. The antecedent of ὅπερ is ψήφισμα, and the relative is the subject of καθαιρεθείη, which is the verb of the protasis of an embedded potential condition in indirect discourse after προύχονται. Hence (somewhat clumsily for English), "if which should be repealed, they claim particularly that there would be no war." μὴ ἂν instead of οὐκ ἂν is peculiar. See **139.1**.

μήδε . . . ὑπολίπησθε. Prohibitive subjunctive (Sm. §1840) parallel to the preceding μὴ νομίσῃ. Hence, "Do not have any lingering thought of regret."

ὡς διὰ μικρὸν ἐπολεμήσατε. This clause gives the putative reason for regret. Sm. §§2240–41. διὰ μικρόν [over a trivial matter] refers to the Megarian Decree.

140.5. τὸ γὰρ βραχύ τι τοῦτο [for this little something] picks up the διὰ μικρόν from the previous sentence. Thus, the little matter of the Megarian Decree is the testing ground of the Athenians' resolve.

οἷς refers to the Spartans.

εἰ ξυγχωρήσετε . . . ἐπιταχθήσεσθε. Minatory-monitory condition (or "emotional future"). Sm. §2328.

ὡς . . . ὑπακούσαντες. Here, ὡς occurs with the participle to give the ground of belief—i.e., what the Spartans believe were the Athenians' reasons. Sm. §2086.

προσφέρεσθαι. "behave toward" (plus the dative). LSJ, s.v. προσφέρω B.I.4. Here, the infinitive phrase acts as a noun, the object of κατα-στήσαιτε. Hence, "By standing firm, you would establish the clear principle of [their] behaving toward you on an equal basis." Sm. §1990.

141.1. διανοήθητε. διανοέομαι (always present middle deponent in early writers) is passive deponent in the aorist. Here, the aorist passive imperative has the meaning "decide, make a decision to."

δύναται. When applied to words, the verb δύναμαι is translated "means, signifies" and takes the accusative. LSJ s.v. II.3.

δικαίωσις. "demand based on a claim of right."

πρὸ δίκης. "instead of negotiation or arbitration."

τὴν γὰρ αὐτὴν . . . ἐπιτασσομένη. "A demand from equals imposed on others instead of arbitration, whether very great or very small, means the same slavery"; i.e., slavery is the result whether the demand is trivial or important. For τοῖς πέλας, cf. 32.4.

141.2. γνῶτε has two objects, τὰ δὲ τοῦ πολέμου and the ὡς clause. Hence, "Listen in detail and know our war resources and that we will possess [resources] no weaker than what belongs to the other side." Grammatically, τὰ δὲ τοῦ πολέμου is the object of γνῶτε, but because it kicks off the sentence, it has the flavor of an accusative of respect—hence, "Regarding the matters of the war . . ."

141.4. ἀπὸ τῶν ἰδίων τε ἅμα ἀπόντες καὶ ἀπὸ τῶν αὐτῶν δαπανῶντες καὶ προσέτι καὶ θαλάσσης εἰργόμενοι. Causal participles. Sm. §2064. Hence, "since to mount naval or land campaigns takes them away from their farms and costs their own money and [since] they are barred from the sea [by Athenian naval power]."

141.5. αἱ δὲ περιουσίαι τοὺς πολέμους μᾶλλον ἢ αἱ βίαιοι ἐσφοραὶ ἀνέχουσιν. "Surpluses [of money], rather than forced taxation, sustain wars." The Athenians have accumulated a war chest, whereas the Spartans will be forced to raise money by special assessments.

τὸ μὲν πιστὸν . . . προαναλώσειν. Τὸ μὲν refers to σῶμα, τὸ δὲ to χρῆμα. The adjectives πιστόν and βέβαιον are predicative. Hence, "having in their bodies something that is reliable, but having in their money something that is insecure." The infinitives are accusatives of respect, specifying in what respect bodies are reliable and in what respect money is not. ἐκ τῶν κινδύνων κἂν περιγενέσθαι means "[reliable] in the fact that it would survive [from out of] the dangers." ἂν marks this infinitive as a transformed potential optative. The infinitive phrase μὴ οὐ προαναλώσειν has μὴ οὐ because of the preceding negative in οὐ βέβαιον. Sm. §§2745–47. Hence, "[not secure] with respect to its not going to be spent before [the war is over]"; i.e., it is not sure that it will not be spent.

141.6. μὴ πρὸς ὁμοίαν ἀντιπαρασκευήν. The negative μή has the force of εἰ μή, "except." Sm. §2346a. It negates the πρὸς ὁμοίαν ἀντιπαρασκευήν—hence, "except against similar counterpreparations," i.e., except against an enemy with the same resources as themselves.

ὅταν. "so long as." ὅταν usually introduces a general temporal clause, but it seems to have causal meaning here; i.e., the Peloponnesians are incapable so long as they do not meet emergencies by means of using a single unified council and so long as each contingent consults its own interest. But "so long as" drifts over into "since." μήτε goes with ἐπιτελῶσι (not with the participle) and is matched in the positive by πάντες τε. By a *constructio ad sensum*, "all" becomes "each," and the verb is singular with ἕκαστος σπεύδῃ.

φιλεῖ μηδέν. The verb is impersonal—in the sense "it usually happens"—with γίγνεσθαι. LSJ s.v. φιλέω II.2. The infinitive phrase μηδὲν ἐπιτελὲς γίγνεσθαι, then, is the grammatical subject of φιλεῖ, and the regular negative for an infinitive not in indirect discourse is μή. Sm. §2711.

141.7. χρόνιοι. "at infrequent intervals, rarely."

ἐν βραχεῖ μὲν μορίῳ. "a small portion [of the time of any meeting together]." The preposition ἐν serves also for τῷ δὲ πλείονι (μορίῳ).

παρὰ τὴν ἑαυτοῦ ἀμέλειαν. παρά here means "resulting from, owing to," a sense used specifically of the margin by which an event occurs, i.e., the sufficient cause. LSJ s.v. C.III.7. Hence, "Each one does not think that there will be harm owing to his own negligence." βλάψειν is used absolutely.

μέλειν δέ τινι καὶ ἄλλῳ ὑπὲρ ἑαυτοῦ τι προϊδεῖν continues the indirect discourse. Still after οἴεται. "but [thinks] that it is the concern of someone else, in his stead, to look after anything." ὑπέρ means "except for, instead of." LSJ s.v. A.II.2. For the position of καί, cf. Thuc. I.70.1.

τῷ αὐτῷ ὑπὸ ἁπάντων ἰδίᾳ δοξάσματι. "by means of the same opinion [being held] on a private basis by everybody." ἰδίᾳ is adverbial. The "same opinion" is the notion that just preceded, namely, that it is somebody else's responsibility to be concerned with the common purpose.

ὥστε . . . λανθάνειν τὸ κοινὸν ἁθρόον φθειρόμενον. λανθάνειν takes the supplementary participle φθειρόμενον (it behaves like τυγχάνω with the participle). Sm. §2096. Hence, "with the result that it escapes [their] notice that the common purpose is being corrupted as a whole." ἀθρόον is predicative.

142.1. ὅταν here has causal meaning. Cf. **141.6.**

σχολῇ is the opposite of ταχύ. Hence, "so long as they delay by providing it slowly."

μενετοί. Verbal adjective built on μένω. Such adjectives in ⁻το⁻ are usually passive, but this one is active. Sm. §472c. Hence, "Opportunities do not wait around."

142.2. ἐπιτείχεσις. This noun and the verb ἐπιτειχίζω refer to building a fortified position within the enemy's boundaries (as the Spartans eventually did at Decelea). The adjective ἄξιον agrees with the nearer of the two elements. Sm. §1030.

142.3. τὴν μὲν γὰρ . . . ἀντεπιτετειχισμένων. τήν should refer to ἐπιτείχεσις; then, πόλιν ἀντίπαλον would be in apposition to it, and the sentence would read "it is difficult to prepare a fortification in enemy territory—that is, an opponent city—even in peacetime." ἀντίπαλος means "equal to an opponent" and here seems to mean something like "a city to balance in opposition." But it makes no sense that such a "city" should be constructed in peacetime, so we must take the term "city" to be a kind of exaggeration. The ἦ of ἦ που δή is asseverative, and the combination, meaning "indeed, forsooth," is used to mark an a fortiori argument. Denniston, *Gr. Part.*², 281. Hence, "indeed far more difficult in wartime." The a fortiori argument has, then, a further emphasis, οὐχ ἧσσον ἐκείνοις—hence, "and no less [difficult] for them [the Spartans] when we have established fortified positions in their territory in return." Gomme (ad loc.) takes τήν as standing for ἐπιτείχεσις and as the object of παρασκευάσασθαι (which he reads), and he proposes the emendation ⟨πρὸς⟩ πόλιν ἀντίπαλον. He translates, "it is a difficult matter to carry out an ἐπιτείχεσις against a city of equal strength even in peacetime, let alone in war." The interpretation of this passage remains obscure.

142.4. εἰ ποιήσονται . . . βλάπτοιεν ἄν. Mixed condition. The protasis is a real condition with future, and the apodosis is a potential optative. Hence, "If they really intend to establish a garrison, they would harm [only] some part of the land."

καταδρομαῖς καὶ αὐτομολίαις. "by incursions and by [encouraging] desertions." αὐτομολία refers here to the desertions of runaway slaves.

οὐχ ἱκανὸν ἔσται ἐπιτειχίζειν τε κωλύειν. The basic construction is οὐχ
ἱκανὸν ἔσται κωλύειν ἡμᾶς, and κωλύειν is followed by the two infinitives ἐπιτειχίζειν and ἀμύνεσθαι, which are connected by τε... καὶ.
Sm. §1993. πλεύσαντας modifies ἡμᾶς. Hence, "it [i.e., the Spartan garri-
son] is not enough to prevent us from sailing to their territory, building
fortifications [there], and attacking with our navy, which is our strength."
ἀμύνεσθαι here means not just "defend ourselves" but, rather, "retaliate."
LSJ s.v. B.II.

142.5. πλέον γὰρ ἡμεῖς ἔχομεν κτλ. It is necessary to sort out the genitives. ἐμπειρίας goes with πλέον to mean "more experience." Sm. §1314.
The brachylogy τοῦ κατὰ γῆν (πολέμου) defines ἐμπειρία. Hence, "we
have more of experience of [warfare] on land out of naval [warfare]
than..." Then, by change of construction, ἐμπειρία... ἐς τὰ ναυτικὰ
means "experience toward naval matters." Hence, "we have more experience of land warfare as a result of [our experience] in naval [warfare] than
they have experience of naval [warfare] from their [experience] of land
[warfare]."

142.7. ἐξείργασθε. Second plural perfect middle of ἐξεργάζομαι. Hence,
"you have not reached a state of complete accomplishment."

προσέτι οὐδὲ μελετῆσαι ἐασόμενοι. "and in addition not even being
allowed to practice."

142.8. πλήθει ἀμαθίαν θρασύνοντες. "making their ignorance bold by
means of their [momentarily superior] number." The argument is that
against a small squadron, the Spartans might risk an encounter.

πρὸς ὀλίγας ἐφορμούσας. Supply ναῦς. Sm. §1027b. ἐφορμέω means
"lie at anchor, blockade"—not to be confused with ἐφορμάω, "attack."

ἐν τῷ μὴ μελετῶντι. Neuter participle with article serving as an abstract
noun. Hence, "in their lack of practice." Sm. §1153b.N2.

142.9. τέχνης ἐστίν. "is a matter of skill." τέχνης is a so-called pregnant
genitive. Cf. 83.2. Smyth calls such a construction a "genitive of quality."
Sm. §1320.

ὅταν τύχῃ. "whenever it chances, casually."

ἐκ παρέργου. "in spare time."

μηδὲν ἐκείνῳ πάρεργον ἄλλο γίγνεσθαι is the subject of ἐνδέχεται. μηδὲν is a redundant negative. Sm. §2739 ff. Hence, "It is not possible for there to be any other spare-time activity with it [naval expertise]." Thus, learning naval warfare is a full-time job, which cannot be practiced as a hobby, and indeed, when practiced full-time, it leaves no time for anything else.

143.1. εἴ τε καί. τε links this condition with those that have gone before. καί here means "also." Hence, "And if they also . . ." Denniston, Gr. Part.², 305.

κινήσαντες τῶν . . . χρημάτων. Κινέω plus the genitive means "apply something (here, the money) to an alien purpose." LSJ s.v. I.2. Cf. Thuc. II.24.1, VI.70.4. τῶν αὐτῶν χρημάτων is a partitive genitive.

μὴ ὄντων . . . μετοίκων. Genitive absolute with negative μή serving as a second protasis. Hence, "If they should try . . . and if we were not equal . . . it would be terrible." The first protasis, εἰ with optative, is potential; the second is in the form of a genitive absolute representing a contrary-to-fact protasis; and the apodosis, imperfect plus ἄν, is contrary-to-fact. Embedded in the μὴ ὄντων genitive absolute is the circumstantial participle ἐσβάντων, signifying means. Sm. §2063. Hence, "if we were not equal by means of going aboard ourselves and our metics going aboard." Thus, the Athenians argue that without the foreign mercenaries (τοὺς ξένους), they have enough among themselves and their metics to do the job. The αὐτῶν stands for ἡμῶν αὐτῶν.

τόδε τε ὑπάρχει. I.e., the fact that the Athenians are equal (ἀντίπαλοι). ὅδε usually looks forward (meaning "the following") but can occasionally refer backward to something just mentioned. Sm. §1247.

143.2. ἐπὶ τῷ κινδύνῳ. "on condition of the risk." LSJ s.v. ἐπί B.III.3.

δέξαιτο. δέχομαι, occurring here with the infinitives φεύγειν and ξυναγωνίζεσθαι, means "accept the offer to, decide to, prefer to." LSJ s.v. I.1.

τὴν . . . αὐτοῦ [πόλιν] φεύγειν. "be exiled from his own city." Sm. §1027b.

ὀλίγων ἡμερῶν . . . δόσεως. δόσεως is the object of the preposition ἕνεκα. μεγάλου μισθοῦ is an objective genitive dependent on δόσις— hence, "a gift of a large wage." ὀλίγων ἡμερῶν is a genitive of measure (Sm. §1325) dependent on μισθοῦ—hence, "a gift of a large wage of a few days." It is unusual for ἕνεκα to precede its object (Sm. §1665a), but see Thuc. I.57.4.

143.3. τὰ δὲ ἡμέτερα . . . ἀπηλλάχθαι (δοκεῖ). ἀπηλλάχθαι is the middle perfect infinitive of ἀπαλλάσσω, which here means "escape, avoid, be free of a charge." LSJ s.v. B.II.6. Hence, "Our situation seems to be free of the [difficulties] with which I have charged them."

οὐκ ἀπὸ τοῦ ἴσου. "not equally [but far better]." This litotes refers here to the superior Athenian navy.

143.4. καὶ οὐκέτι ἐκ τοῦ ὁμοίου ἔσται . . . καί. "will turn out to be more serious . . . than." The argument is that if the Spartans invade the Athenians' land, the Athenians will attack by sea, and the devastation of part of the Peloponnesus will be more serious to the Spartans strategically than the devastation of all of Attica would be to Athens. For καί as a comparative particle, see Sm. §2875.

ἀντιλαβεῖν. "take as a substitute." ἄλλην stands for ἄλλην γῆν. Sm. §1027b.

143.5. ὅτι ἐγγύτατα τούτου διανοηθέντας. "putting ourselves in a frame of mind as close as possible to this [idea]"—sc., that the Athenians were islanders. Sm. §§345, 1086.

ἀφεῖναι. Aorist active infinitive of ἀφίημι.

χρὴ . . . ὀργισθέντας . . . μὴ διαμάχεσθαι. "It is necessary that you not fight out of anger."

πολλῷ πλείοσι modifies Πελοποννησίοις and means "who are more numerous by far."

κρατήσαντες . . . προαπόλλυται. κρατήσαντες is a conditional participle. Sm. §2067. Hence, "For if we win, we will fight again against undiminished numbers [because fighting the Peloponnesians on land gives them an inexhaustible advantage of numbers]." καὶ ἢν σφαλῶμεν is parallel with the conditional participle—hence, "And if we lose . . ." τὰ τῶν ξυμμάχων . . . προσαπόλλυται means "our allies will be lost in addition." προσαπόλλυται, though present, is parallel with the future μαχούμεθα and has future force. "The present is used instead of the future in statements of what is immediate, likely, certain, or threatening" (Sm. §1879). τὰ τῶν ξυμμάχων refers back to ἄλλα οὐκ ἀπὸ τοῦ ἴσου μεγάλα in I.143.3—hence, "the great advantages of [having] allies."

τήν τε ὀλόφυρσιν μὴ . . . ποιεῖσθαι (χρή). This negative infinitive is dependent on the preceding χρή. Hence, "It is necessary to make lamentation not over houses and land but, rather, over [the loss of] men."

αὐτά. I.e., fields and houses.

144.1. ἀρχήν τε μὴ ἐπικτᾶσθαι ἅμα πολεμοῦντες. "not to add to the empire during the war." Sm. §2081.

αὐθαιρέτους. "self-chosen, self-incurred, brought on oneself."

144.2. ἐν ἄλλῳ λόγῳ ἅμα τοῖς ἔργοις. "in another speech when events warrant"—literally, "at the time of the events." Sm. §1701.

ξενηλασίας. Curiously, this is mentioned here for the first time. The Spartans expelled non-Spartans from Lacedaemon from time to time. Cf. Xen. Lac. 14.4; Ar. Av. 1013–16.

οὔτε γὰρ ἐκεῖνο κωλύει ἐν ταῖς σπονδαῖς οὔτε τόδε. οὐ κωλύει is equivalent to οὐδὲν κωλύει. Hence, "nothing in the truce forbids either this or that." τόδε refers to the Megarian Decree, ἐκεῖνο to ξενηλασία. Ordinarily, ἐκεῖνο refers to the more remote matter mentioned (Sm. §1261), which would here be the Megarian Decree, mentioned first. But in this instance, ἐκεῖνο seems to refer to the policy of the more remote state, namely, Sparta, while τόδε refers to the policy of the nearer Athenians.

εἰ καὶ αὐτονόμους ἔχοντες ἐσπεισάμεθα. Real condition (not contrary-to-fact) in the past. Hence, "if [in fact] we made the truce while having them autonomous." English would prefer to reverse the emphasis and say, "if in fact they were autonomous at the time we made the truce." The point is, of course, ironic.

μὴ σφίσι ἐπιτηδείως αὐτονομεῖσθαι. "to be autonomous not in a manner convenient to themselves"—i.e., ironically, whenever the Spartans let their cities become democratic instead of oligarchical. The scholiast argues that the τοῖς Λακεδαιμονίοις of the MSS is no more than a gloss on σφίσι that has crept from the margin into the text.

ἀλλ᾽ αὐτοῖς ἑκάστοις ὡς βούλονται. "but [conveniently] to themselves each, as they wish."

144.3. εἰδέναι δὲ χρή takes three ὅτι clauses.

ὅτι ἀνάγκη (ἐστί) πολεμεῖν
(ὅτι) . . . ἕξομεν
ὅτι . . . περιγίγνονται

The ἢν δεχώμεθα clause is dependent on ἕξομεν. It is an eventual condition with future apodosis (future-more-vivid condition) embedded in a ὅτι clause after εἰδέναι. The object of δεχώμεθα is the implied πολεμεῖν. ἧσσον ἐγκεισομένους means "about to press less hard." LSJ s.v. ἔγκειμαι II. Hence, "we will find them less eager to fight."

οὐκ ἀπὸ τοσῶνδε. "not from so great resources."

ὧν. Sc., πατέρων. In the middle, λείπεσθαι means "fall short of, be inferior to" and takes the genitive. LSJ s.v. λείπω B.II.3. For οὐ χρή instead of χρὴ μή, see Sm. §2714. χρή takes either οὐ or μή.

145. οὐδὲν κελευόμενοι ποιήσειν. Indirect discourse after ἀπεκρίναντο. Hence, "that they would do nothing on demand."

146. ἐν αὐταῖς. Understand σπονδαῖς.

ἀκηρύκτως. "without heralds." If the war had actually broken out, they could only communicate by means of heralds, so this is an indication that the war had not yet commenced.

σπονδῶν γὰρ κτλ. This γάρ clause explains why there was suspicion— because such events (τὰ γιγνόμενα) were tantamount to a breaking of the truce and a reason for war.

SELECTED BIBLIOGRAPHY

❧

GENERAL INTRODUCTIONS TO THUCYDIDES

Cawkwell, G. *Thucydides and the Peloponnesian War*. London and New York: Routledge, 1997.

Connor, W. R. *Thucydides*. Princeton: Princeton University Press, 1984.

Cornford, F. M. *Thucydides Mythistoricus*. London: Arnold, 1907.

de Ste. Croix, G. E. M. *The Origins of the Peloponnesian War*. London: Duckworth, 1972.

Finley, John H., Jr. *Thucydides*. 2d ed. Cambridge: Harvard University Press, 1947.

Kagan, D. *The Archidamian War*. Ithaca: Cornell University Press, 1974.

Luce, T. J. *The Greek Historians*. London and New York: Routledge, 1997.

Rawlings, H. R. *The Structure of Thucydides' History*. Princeton: Princeton University Press, 1981.

Stadter, Philip, ed. *The Speeches of Thucydides*. Chapel Hill: University of North Carolina Press, 1973.

Strassler, R. B., ed. *The Landmark Thucydides: A Comprehensive Guide to the Peloponnesian War*. With translation by Richard Crawley. New York: Free Press, 1996.

COMMENTARIES

Classen, J., and J. Steup. *Thukydides erklärt von J. Classen*. 5th ed. revised by J. Steup. Vol. 1, *Einleitung. Erstes Buch*. Berlin: Weidmannsche Buchhandlung, 1919.

141

Gomme, A. W. A *Historical Commentary on Thucydides*. Vol. 1, *Introduction and Commentary on Book I*. Oxford: Clarendon, 1956.

Hornblower, Simon. *A Commentary on Thucydides*. Vol. 1. Oxford: Clarendon, 1991.

Marchant, E. C. *Thucydides Book I*. 1905. Reprint, with a new introduction and bibliography by Thomas Wiedemann, Bristol: Bristol Classical Press, 1982.

GREEK GRAMMARS AND GRAMMATICAL WORKS

Buck, C. D. *Comparative Grammar of Greek and Latin*. Chicago: University of Chicago Press, 1933.

Chantraine, P. *La formation des noms en grec ancien*. Paris: Klincksieck, 1933, reprinted 1979.

Denniston, J. D. *The Greek Particles*. 2d ed. Oxford: Clarendon, 1954.

Goodwin, W. W. *Greek Grammar*. Revised by C. B. Gulick. New York: Ginn and Company, 1930.

———. *Syntax of the Moods and Tenses of the Greek Verb*. Boston: Ginn and Company, 1890.

Kühner, R. *Ausführliche Grammatik der Griechischen Sprache*. Part 2, *Satzlehre*. 2 vols. revised by Bernhard Gerth. Hannover and Leipzig: Hahnsche Buchhandlung, 1898. Reprinted Munich: Max Huebner Verlag, 1963.

Schwyzer, Eduard. *Griechische Grammatik*. Vol. 1, *Allgemeine Teil, Lautlehre, Wortbildung, Flexion*. 3d ed. Munich: C. H. Beck'sche Verlagsbuchhandlung, 1959. Vol. 2, *Syntax und Syntaktische Stilistik*, 2d ed. completed and edited by Albert Debrunner. Munich: C. H. Beck'sche Verlagsbuchhandlung, 1959.

Smyth, Herbert Weir. *Greek Grammar*. Revised by Gordon Messing. Cambridge: Harvard University Press, 1956.

LEXICA

Liddell, H. G., and Robert Scott. *A Greek–English Lexicon*. Revised by Sir Henry Stuart Jones with the assistance of Roderick McKenzie, with a supplement. Oxford: Clarendon, 1968.

———. *A Lexicon Abridged from Liddell and Scott's Greek–English Lexicon*. Oxford: Clarendon, 1891.

TEXTS

Stuart Jones, H. *Thucydidis Historiae*. Edited by Henry Stuart Jones, revised by J. E. Powell. 2 vols. Oxford: Clarendon, 1942.

TRANSLATIONS

Crawley, Richard, trans. *The Peloponnesian War,* by Thucydides. Revised by T. E. Wick. New York: Modern Library, 1982.

Lattimore, Stephen, trans. *The Peloponnesian War,* by Thucydides. Indianapolis: Hacket, 1998.

Warner, Rex, trans. *History of the Peloponnesian War,* by Thucydides. With introductions and notes by M. I. Finley. Harmondsworth: Penguin Books, 1954. Reprint, 1972.

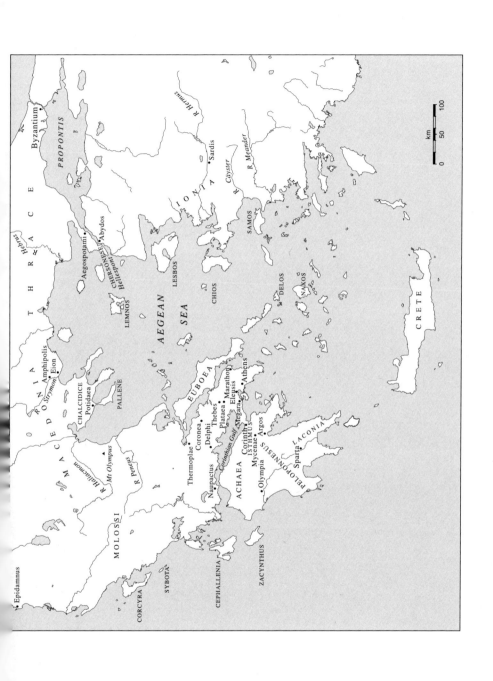